APPLE BACKPACK:
Humanized Programming in BASIC

by

Scot Kamins, Ph.D.
and
Mitchell Waite

- Crashproofing Programs
- User Help Menu Methods
- Applesoft BASIC Examples
- Software Documentation Techniques
- Screen Text Presentation, Verification
- Demo Programs: STATES & CAPITALS, ELECTRONIC PHONE PAD

BYTE Books
A Subsidiary of McGraw-Hill
Peterborough, NH 03458

Library of Congress Cataloging in Publication Data

Kamins, Scot.
Apple backpack.

Includes index.
1. Apple II (Computer)--Programming.
2. Basic (Computer program language)
I. Waite, Mitchell. II. Title.
QA76.8.A662K35 001.64'2 82-4238
ISBN 0-07-033356-4 AACR2

Edited by Bruce Roberts.
Design and Production Supervision by Ellen Klempner.
Drawings by Bob Johnson.
Production Editing by Tom McMillan.
Production by Mike Lonsky.
Typesetting by Valerie Horn.
Printed and Bound by Halliday Lithograph Corp.
Arcata Company
North Quincy, Massachusetts.

DEDICATION PAGE

the finer parts of this work are dedicated to

BRUCE TOGNAZZINI

who helped humanize my earliest programs

. . . *Scot Kamins*

ACKNOWLEDGEMENTS

The authors would like to give their thanks to the following people who participated in the initial development of the seeds of this Apple Backpack.

Dr. Malcolm McAffee
Dr. Lou Caillat
Dr. Arlen Wilson
Sam Bassett
Warren Harmon
Dean Gengle

For their help in reviewing and analyzing the manuscript the authors would like to give their appreciation to the following experts.

David Fox
Julie Ann Arca
Patrick M. Burnstad
Annie Fox
Philip Lieberman
John Angermeyer

Finally we would like to pay respect to David Fox and Julie Ann Arca for their valuable involvement in the final manuscript review. We would like to thank David for his analysis of the BASIC code and bug killing and Julie for her valuable critiques.

Scot Kamins
Mitchell Waite

TABLE OF CONTENTS

PREFACE

If you want to write programs that are designed for people to use, then this is the book for you. *APPLE BACKPACK: Humanized Programming in BASIC* was written to help stamp out code that ignores the humanity of people who use computers. This *Backpack* is about writing programs that are user-friendly in the BASIC language.

Far too many programs in the new world of personal computer software "crash" easily, are confusing, and leave the person using the program totally in the dark. Using real working examples that can be included in your own programs immediately, this book teaches you how to write friendly BASIC programs loaded with pro-human features. The *Backpack* shows step by step (and in a very human way) how to write code that works *with* the operator—a process we call *humanized programming*.

Many of the secrets and programming tricks of today's computer specialists are included. While all the examples are written in the popular Applesoft BASIC, any programmer who codes in Microsoft BASIC will find that only simple modifications will be necessary to make the examples run in whatever computer is being used. Owners of the IBM, Xerox, Atari, PET, and TRS computers will find the *Backpack* especially valuable as a handbook of practical, friendly programming techniques.

We expect our readers to have *some* familiarity with BASIC, and while it certainly will enhance learning to have a microcomputer handy, it isn't necessary to have a computer to appreciate this book.

The Introduction provides a framework for the book and tells what humanized programming is about. You'll read about the sordid history of anti-human programming and why (up to now) microcomputer programs seem to have been written only for other programmers. We'll go over the difference between yesterday's and today's microcomputer users. We'll talk about computers as well-trained, low-profile servants. And finally, we'll give you some tips on how to get the most out of this book.

Chapter 1, Screen Formatting for Clarity, shows how to design inviting title pages that make the user want to continue with the program. You'll learn concepts of text presentation that tell you not only how to present text in the most human ways, but why those ways are best. You'll practice techniques for centering, blocking, and highlighting text, as well as how to make text and numbers line up on the screen, whether at the left edge, right edge, or any place in between!

Chapter 2, Crashproofing Programs, covers protecting programs from "bombing out." The most common (as well as a few uncommon) user violations and the best ways to handle them are covered, and we show how to avoid getting your beautifully formatted screens messed up by "BAD INPUT: RE-ENTER?" messages. You'll learn how to use strings for all inputs, including numbers, and why you ought to do so. And you'll find a bunch of tricks for reducing the likelihood of user errors through the use of numeric menus.

Chapter 3, Verifications and Validations, tells how to set up BASIC programs that recognize the tendency of human beings to say things they don't mean. This chapter helps you write code that lets the operator change his or her mind about what was typed in answer to an input request. We cover such pro-human features as auto-typing (making the computer, instead of the operator, do repetitive typing) and OK checkers (entry verifications). And we show how to make your on-screen prompts clear and concise.

Chapter 4, Directions on the Display, demonstrates how to put instructions for using the program into the program itself. This really exciting concept, called *user help menus*, provides a friendly and highly humanized interaction between the operator and the computer. You'll learn what information to store in random-access memory (RAM) and what directions to keep on the disk (and *how* to use the disk drive to do it). And we'll give some pointers on such tricky types of input as dates and telephone numbers.

Chapter 5, Hard Copy Documentation, explains the ground rules for writing good manuals specifically designed to go with interactive software. We've included detailed instructions on such documentation aids as Tables of Contents, Glossaries, Indexes, and Reference Cards. You'll also see how to tell your programs' operators about Fatal Error Warnings and Crash Recovery Instructions. And as a bonus, so that you can reap the benefits of your highly humanized program, there's a special section on how to obtain copyright protection.

There are three Appendices. The first one is an ASCII code chart to make doing fancy programming easier. The remaining two are Applesoft BASIC listings of two immediately useful programs written especially for this book that demonstrate all the humanizing concepts the book presents. STATES & CAPITALS is a fun-to-use educational game that can be modified to teach almost anything. ELECTRONIC PHONE PAD is a specialized disk-based program for storing and retrieving telephone messages in a fairly sophisticated way. It can serve as the central message-taking center for a regular business office. It has all the features of a truly user-friendly program. A complete manual for the program is contained in the appendix so that you can really ‘‘see’’ what good software documentation looks like.

Scot Kamins
Mitchell Waite

I WISH YOU COULD TALK— I'D LOVE TO KNOW WHAT YOU'RE THINKING
I WISH YOU COULD THINK— I'D LOVE TO KNOW WHAT YOU'RE SAYING

INTRODUCTION

As personal computers become more and more popular, more non-technical people will have computers in their homes. These non-programming computer users will want software that, of course, runs right every time. But they also want programs that are people-oriented and it is unlikely they will bother with programs that are *not*. Writing people-oriented code is what humanized programming is all about.

WHAT IS HUMANIZED PROGRAMMING?

Humanized programming is an attitude toward writing "interactive" code for microcomputers that puts major emphasis on communication with the user. It stresses above all else the human interface, or the way the computer seeks information from and delivers information to the computer user. Humanized programming is not so much concerned with processing as it is with interactive input and output techniques for microcomputers. This book is the first teaching manual for those techniques.

A Look at Yesterday

In the past, programmers of home computers spent almost no time teaching their computers how to behave with humans. Their main concerns were to get the program working (that is, get it to process data without crashing too often) and to get it out on the market. There was virtually no concern about how user-friendly the program was. The programmers' attitude seemed to be "if *we* can figure out how to work it, people who use it ought to be able to do so as well." They tended to write code that had little screen prompting, few directions, and almost no error trapping. Their codes paid precious little attention to how information appeared on the screen (the aesthetics of screen display). All too often the program bombed when least expected.

These programmers perceived humanizing stuff (like error trapping and attractive screen displays) as unnecessary if they considered it at all. Nearly all early micro users were also programmers who, being highly sophisticated users, tended not to make beginner's errors in using programs and could fathom fairly quickly how to get through a program without lots of help. These smart users were more concerned with processes—how a particular problem was solved in terms of the code itself, or how elegant the code was, or how clever. How friendly the program was or how easy it was to use just didn't enter into the picture.

Many early programmers were professionals who had been writing on mainframes (giant IBMs and other dinosaurs) and their programs were being used by other computer operators steeped in computer usage. *These computer operators learned to talk with computers in various shorthands that were machine-centered as opposed to human-centered.* Computer memory on the mainframes was expensive, so it made better economic sense to have the operators learn to speak the computer's language than to have the machines learn to speak to humans.

When the first personal computers came into being in 1975 and, more particularly, when the second generation of personal computers such as the Apple II appeared in 1977, the old economic constraints no longer applied. Computers came down so low in price that non-technical people began to try to use them. Computer memory dropped in price from dollars per unit to pennies per unit to millicents per unit, and it became economically feasible for computers to be programmed with humans in mind.

The programmers of the world, however, were apparently not as ready for humans as the new machines were. The technologists had not yet caught up with their own technology! Programmers, even on the microcomputers, continued to write as if they had to serve the no-longer-existing economic restrictions of their computers. This unfortunate attitude still exists today.

Where are we today?

Today's computer users are a different breed. Most of them are decidedly not computer whizzes, and don't want to be. They are doctors, lawyers, teachers, students, and, in general, just everyday folks with an enthusiastic curiosity towards computers. They see their machines as tools to solve particular problems. They have little interest in figuring out obscure codes, scant directions, syntax errors, "restart from line 27265," or the like. They want to use their computers, not fight with them.

These new computerists are non-technical types, buying computers at the rate of over a thousand per day at their friendly neighborhood computer retail outlets—and the number is steadily climbing. By the beginning of summer, 1981, there were over 250,000 Apple IIs alive and well in homes and offices. The Tandy Corporation had twice that number of TRS-80s in use, and similar figures were coming from other companies. These people form an ever-increasing base for the microcomputer world. Programmers who want to have their products used will have to give serious consideration to the wants and needs of these new computerists. That is where this book comes in. It attempts to make programming more human-responsive for the convenience of today's and tomorrow's computer users.

THE PRIME DIRECTIVE AND HOW TO FILL IT

The prime directive of humanized programming is "Consider the Humanity of the User." The user shouldn't have to know more about a computer than how to use its keyboard (that is, how to be a hunt-and-peck typist). The computer, on the other hand, should make certain assumptions about the user and about the relationship between the two of them:

- The user may not know how to use the computer, and the computer is responsible for teaching the user how to operate it if that becomes necessary.

- The user may forget how to operate a particular program in the middle of the operation, and the computer is obligated to provide help if this should happen.

- The user may enter invalid data (that is, data that might interrupt processing and ordinarily cause a program "crash"), and the computer must trap that data and politely inform the user of the error and prompt for valid data.

- The user may enter incorrect data (data that won't cause the program to go down, but that is untrue—a name in an address field, for instance), and the computer must either validate (confirm) the data before accepting it or must later allow the user to change the data, or both.

- The user, being a human being, has a nervous system that responds to order and clarity. The machine therefore must seek and present information in an orderly and clear manner.

- Users come in different levels of sophistication. The machine must communicate with the user at the user's level.

- Users have an innate tendency to move towards pleasure and away from pain. The machine must always strive to have the user move towards itself by providing a pleasurable, as opposed to painful, experience.

When today's computerist loads a program into the home computer, he or she has the right to expect the machine to act like a well-trained servant. The machine should do much and ask little. When it does ask something, the questions should be clear and brief. Like an excellent waiter who keeps the water glasses filled without being asked, the machine should anticipate the user's needs as much as possible. Above all, the machine should remember at all times that the user is the boss.

APPLE BACKPACK: Humanized Programming in BASIC is a handbook for programmers who want to train computers to be better servants.

HOW TO USE THIS BOOK

Different people have different learning styles and we've tried to accomodate as many as we could in *APPLE BACKPACK: Humanized Programming in BASIC.*

For People Who Like Tutorials

While many people can learn a lot about interactive programming by reading this book cozily snuggled up in front of a fire, the majority of readers will learn more by reading it snuggled up with their computers. Each chapter is filled with examples meant to be typed into your beast as you go along, and the code for each example is described in detail. The chapters are written to follow each other, but each one can be read independently and their examples used without a lot of reference to previous chapters. If you like an orderly process, read the book through from the beginning following the suggestions as you come across them.

For Readers With Immediate Needs

Some readers will have special applications for humanized programming and will want to go directly to the chapter concerned with their immediate need. If you're one of these people, then the following chapter outlines should prove helpful:

1. "Screen Formatting for Clarity" deals with how things look on the computer display. This chapter shows how to format both words and numbers for the most effective communication; how to block, center, and format text to make the most important items stand out, and how to prevent broken words (wraparound) and "runaway" text.

2. "Crashproofing Programs" demonstrates the most effective techniques for preventing program "crashes" due to user errors. There are sections dealing with string length violations and how to prevent them, how to use the ASCII code system for effective error trapping, string as opposed to numeric inputs to prevent wrong-character infractions, and how to limit the characters the computer will accept to keep program "blow-up" possibilities to a minimum.

3. "Verifications and Validations" teaches techniques for helping the operator make sure that the information he or she is typing into the computer is the correct information. Included are ways to help the users correct input mistakes, the extended use of single-

character inputs (the GET statement), setting up various options to correct information, how to verify and reverify what the user types, and how to use on-screen prompts clearly and effectively.

4. "Directions on the Display" shows a variety of ways the programmer can use the computer's screen to help the user get the most out of the program. Step-by-step examples are provided to show how to solicit information concisely and clearly, how to get the user to type what's needed (and *only* what's needed), how to construct forms for the operator to fill out from the computer's keyboard, how to design and construct both brief and extended on-screen help menus, and how to use both random-access memory (RAM) and disk memory to help the user every step of the way.

5. "Hard Copy Documentation" describes how to write solid applications program manuals. There are sections on what topics documentation should include and how to include them, what documentation aids like glossaries and quick reference cards are about, how to write program tutorials and why they are important, what extras like crash-recovery techniques and fatal error warnings to include, how to tell users that your programs are copyrighted, and how to secure those copyrights.

The Appendices include listings of two complete programs written especially for this book showing how a variety of humanized programming techniques can be combined to produce finished pieces. Appendix III includes a complete operator's manual so that you can see how good documentation should look.

For Experimenters and Non-wordy Learners

Some people don't like long explanations and prefer to get right to the heart of the matter. For those folks we have scattered screen listings that demonstrate every technique we talk about throughout the text pages. Type these program lines into your computer and try them out. Modify and embellish them, and mix them with techniques of your own. And by *all* means, try them out in your own programs!

If you want to see how all the techniques described in this book work together, then go right to the appendices and enter STATES & CAPITALS (Appendix II) and/or ELECTRONIC PHONE PAD (Appendix III—see below for a description of these programs). Not only will that help improve your typing skills and keep you off the streets, but you'll also be able to see how a variety of humanized programming techniques are linked together to form cohesive wholes.

For Novel Fans and Conceptual Thinkers

A final technique is to read the book away from the computer, just becoming familiar with the ideas and saving the actual code-entering for later. The book has many screen simulations and drawings showing exactly what effect the sample programs and techniques will have on the computer's display. Besides, the plot is intriguing.

TWO SAMPLE PROGRAMS: STATES & CAPITALS AND ELECTRONIC PHONE PAD (EPP)

The two complete programs we've produced (see Appendix II and Appendix III) are meant to be examples of how completed humanized programs should operate. While neither program is a deathless example of the finest structured coding techniques, both demonstrate very well what writing programs for people is all about.

STATES & CAPITALS, which you'll find in Appendix II, is an educational game. The computer chooses 10 states and presents them one at a time to the player. The player must type in the name of that state's capital. If the capital is right the player is awarded 10 points, accompanied by appropriate bells and whistles—and a cheering section! If it's wrong the computer displays the names of three capitals, one of which is the correct one. If the player chooses the correct one from the list, five points are awarded. If the player is wrong, the computer gets 10 points. Running scores are displayed, as are the names of all states and capitals already guessed. The game can be modified to teach any "matching pairs," and directions on how to do so are included.

ELECTRONIC PHONE PAD (Appendix III) is a disk-based program designed to be used by a receptionist or telephone answering person. Its operator's manual was written for the complete computer novice, and the program is loaded with special "real time" help features. When a telephone call comes in, the operator types significant information about the call (time, caller, return telephone number, who the call is for, what the message is, etc.) into the computer. Later messages can be recalled for review or printout in a variety of ways.

The Program Operator's Manual contains 20 pages of hard copy documentation for ELECTRONIC PHONE PAD and is designed to exemplify the principles of Chapter 5. A full walkthrough (a step-by-step tutorial) of the program is included, as is an operation summary card for easy reference.

LEMON
HUH?
SOB

CHAPTER 1:

SCREEN FORMATTING FOR CLARITY

Screen formatting deals with those techniques that cause text to be displayed on a computer monitor or TV screen (CRT) in an organized way. We believe that it isn't reasonable for a programmer merely to throw characters on a screen in a haphazard fashion. That's OK for grocery lists, but grocery lists don't need to be presented in any particular order or format to make sense.

Although words are meant to convey information, the format and order in which the words are presented may either clarify or cloud totally the words' meaning. This chapter deals with formatting a program's output so that it provides clarity rather than confusion.

We'll cover setting up the title page—the first thing the user sees when your program begins. We'll tell you how to make different elements of your text presentation stand out by using techniques like centering, blocking, and highlighting. You'll learn how to make words, numbers, and decimals "line up"—and how to avoid having words "split down the middle" when they overrun the screen. And you'll find a number of other tips about how to communicate effectively through good screen formatting.

THE TITLE PAGE

For starters, we'll deal with the first thing with which a computer user comes into contact: the title page. Of course, all the techniques discussed here can (and should) be used within the body of a program. It's just more convenient to present them in relation to a title page. The title page is the information which appears on the computer screen when the program is first fired up (started). In this book, a page and a screen are synonymous.

Title pages are likely to contain three major elements—the title of the program (with any related subtitles or brief explanation), a credits section saying who wrote the program and presenting any pertinent copyright information, and instructions about how to get the program started. Some title pages also mention the distributor, some use interesting graphics to create large colored titles, and some start the program process automatically. But to keep things simple, we'll use the definition of three elements outlined above—title, copyright, and start-up instructions.

EXAMPLE
Here's some raw data for the title page of a little computer game (we won't program the whole game in this book. We'll leave that to you). None of the data is formatted. Our job as humanizers of programs is to display information on a CRT in a way that is easy to read and to understand:

world power
the nuclear proliferation game
copyright 1982
the trilateral commission
all rights reserved
press any key to commence fission

Centering aligns information so that it appears balanced and neat on the screen. First, we'll break the data into categories by selectively centering and blocking it.

Centering

Centering is used with titles, section headings, and in general with any word or phrase you want to stand out. The formula for centering on a computer screen is the same for centering on a typewriter sheet: count the number of columns available on the screen, subtract from that number the total number of characters in the word or phrase you want to center, and divide the difference by two. The result is the column number where the first character should be displayed. In our computer's BASIC the code for centering a string is

CENTERING ALGORITHM

```
HTAB ( CT - LEN (PC$) ) / 2
```

where CT holds the total number of columns on your screen and PC$ holds the phrase to be centered. HTAB in our Apple II stands for Horizontal Tab (which is the number of spaces indented from the left hand side of the screen), LEN is BASIC's length function (which gives the number of characters in the string enclosed by parentheses), and the parentheses after HTAB and before the slash (/) insure that the subtraction will take place before the division. We usually use this centering formula as a subroutine, as you'll see in the upcoming program example.

Blocking

Blocking is the process of organizing phrases into pleasing rectangular partitions on the screen. The plain old PRINT statement is used to accomplish this. Used by itself as a BASIC command, PRINT will leave an "empty" line on the screen, separating the data into blocks. It works like the block paragraphing many people study in business English courses. You'd be amazed how this piece of seeming nothing can improve clarity and aesthetics. Here's our title page using both centering and blocking:

```
                    world power

             the nuclear proliferation game






copyright 1982
the trilateral commission
all rights reserved


press any key to commence fission
```

Doesn't this look better than just plopping data anywhere on the display? The title and subtitle are reasonably linked together, as are the credit and copyright lines. The instruction line is separated from the rest of the text, and all three groups stand out as individual packets of information—which they are! Still, it could be better (never satisfied, these humanist types). We need something to give a little pizazz to the title page, to make the sections stand out a bit more...we need highlighting.

Highlighting

Highlighting is a technique to make a character, word, or phrase distinctly different from its companions. Most computers allow some form of highlighting either through the use of upper and lowercase letters (capitals and small), inverse video (black letters on a white background), or colored text on a contrasting-colored background. All computers have some special non-alphanumeric characters (-,?,*,&,%, etc.) that can also be used to make text stand out.

Upper/lower case can be used most effectively for clarity and attractive printing. Of course, they should be used in conformity to the laws of good grammar while still allowing for personal creativity. If e.e. cummings can get away with it....

In our title page, for instance, we might put the title in all upper case and the subtitle in just initial upper case. Those lines would look like this:

WORLD POWER

The Nuclear Proliferation Game

And following the rules, we would also put the initial letters of the authoring groups in caps:

copyright 1982
The Trilateral Commission

And just to be snazzy, we could use a special character like the hyphen and an empty space or two to make the next line stand out:

- all rights reserved -

Let's also put a few dots at the end of the instruction line:

press any key to commence...

Machines that don't have upper and lower case but do have inverse video can use that function in the same place we've used capitals. In our Apple II, for instance, we can use the command POKE 50, 63 to make all characters printed to the screen come up in black-on-white; when we want to go back to normal output (that is, white letters on a black background), we use the command POKE 50, 255. Our Applesoft language supports the commands INVERSE and NORMAL to do the same thing as the POKEs.

> POKE is a command that puts into a specific memory location a particular number. POKE 50, 63 puts into memory location 50 the number 63. Location 50 in the Apple controls in what mode characters are to be displayed on the screen (white-on-black, black-on-white, or flashing), and the number 63 tells the computer to use inverse video. Not all computers have the POKE command; check your computer's manual.

Text Justification

We would add one more feature to our title page: right justification of the credits section. To right justify is to line up the last letters of lines, as opposed to lining up the first letters (left justify). We've been left justifying all along since our computers do it for us automatically. A carriage return puts the cursor at the first column—which is to say, in the left justify position. We can left justify on our own by using the TAB command: everything that's printed at TAB (24) will be lined up at the 24th column of the screen. Later in this chapter we'll cover justifying numbers.

The formula for right justification is essentially the same as the formula for centering but without the division step:

RIGHT JUSTIFICATION ALGORITHM

HTAB CT – LEN (RJ$)

where RJ$ is the phrase to be right justified and CT represents the available number of character positions on a line (usually 40, 64, or 80 depending on the computer or terminal configuration). Like the centering formula, we keep this tucked away as a subroutine. In computers where a carriage return and line feed are issued automatically when the last column on a line is displayed, the formula must be altered slightly:

RIGHT JUSTIFICATION WITH AUTO LINEFEED AND CARRIAGE RETURN

HTAB CT – 1 – LEN (RJ$)

In this situation we subtract one from the column total so that we don't end up with extra blank lines on the screen. Try both formulas in your machine to see which works best.

Putting all these techniques together the title page should look like this:

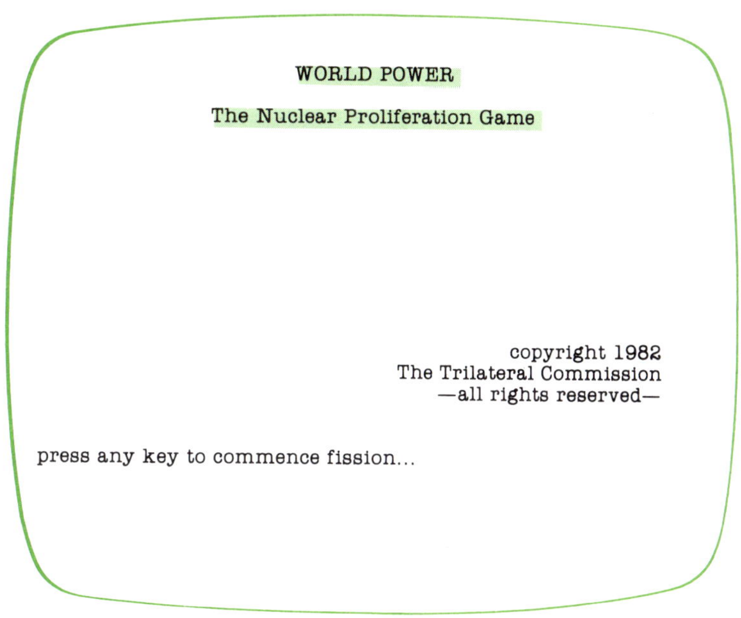

Here's the code for the whole title page. It will run directly on an Apple II with Applesoft BASIC:

Listing 1.1

```
0   REM  "AESTHETIC" TITLE PAGE DEMO
1   REM DEMONSTRATES CENTERING, RIGHT JUSTIFICATION,
    HIGHLIGHTING
5   HOME : REM CLEAR THE SCREEN
10 CT = 40: REM SCREEN WIDTH
20 PC$ = "WORLD POWER"
30  PRINT
40  GOSUB 1000: REM CENTERING
50  PRINT
60 PC$ = "THE NUCLEAR PROLIFERATION GAME"
70  GOSUB 1000
80  VTAB 15: REM SET VERTICAL POSITION
90 RJ$ = "COPYRIGHT 1980"
100  GOSUB 2000: REM RIGHT JUSTIFY
110 RJ$ = "THE TRILATERAL COMMISSION"
120  GOSUB 2000: REM  RIGHT JUSTIFY
130 RJ$ = "- ALL RIGHTS RESERVED -"
140  GOSUB 2000
150  VTAB 20
160  PRINT "PRESS ANY KEY TO COMMENCE FISSION..."
999  END
1000  REM CENTERING ROUTINE
1010  HTAB (CT -  LEN (PC$)) / 2
1020  INVERSE : REM SET BLACK-ON-WHITE
1030  PRINT PC$
1040  NORMAL : REM SET WHITE-ON-BLACK
1050  RETURN
2000  REM RIGHT JUSTIFY ROUTINE
2010  HTAB CT - 1 -  LEN (RJ$)
2020  PRINT RJ$
2030  RETURN
```

Bordering

If you want to get even fancier, you can experiment with bordering. In this technique you use a special character repeatedly to make a box around some phrase or whole screen of text to make it stand out. If we want to border the program title using the dollar sign as a special character appropriate to the game's subject matter, our title would look like this:

```
$$$$$$$$$$$$$$$
$             $
$ WORLD POWER $
$             $
$$$$$$$$$$$$$$$
```

Here's a short program that will let you experiment with different border "characters." You can adopt the code to use in your own programs if you like the idea of bordering as a highlighting technique:

Listing 1.2

```
0   REM TITLE BOXING DEMO
1   REM  DEMONSTRATES HIGHLIGHTING THROUGH THE USE
    OF BORDERS
5   REM
10   HOME : REM CLEAR THE SCREEN
20  TITLE$ = "WORLD POWER": REM USE WHATEVER TITLE
    YOU LIKE
30   INPUT "WHAT BORDER CHARACTER SHALL I USE?
     ";CHARACTER$
35   IF CHARACTER$ = "S" THEN  END : REM ENTER "S"
     TO STOP
40   GOSUB 1000: REM PRINT TOP BORDER
50   GOSUB 2000: REM PRINT SIDE BORDER
60   REM HERE COMES A SIDE BORDER, A SPACE,
     THE TITLE, ETC.
70   PRINT CHARACTER$;" ";TITLE$;" ";CHARACTER$
80   GOSUB 2000: REM PRINT ANOTHER SIDE
90   GOSUB 1000: REM PRINT BOTTOM BORDER
100   PRINT
110   GOTO 20
1000   REM THIS SECTION PRINTS THE TOP BORDER
1010   FOR X = 1 TO  LEN (TITLE$) + 4
1020   PRINT CHARACTER$;
1030   NEXT X
1040   PRINT
1050   RETURN
2000   REM THIS SECTION PRINTS THE SIDE BORDERS
       WITH BLANKS AS FILLER
2010   PRINT CHARACTER$;
2020   FOR X = 1 TO  LEN (TITLE$) + 2
2030   PRINT " ";
2040   NEXT X
2050   PRINT CHARACTER$
2060   RETURN
```

The adventurous among you will discover how to border the entire title page for added fanciness.

ABOUT AESTHETIC APPROPRIATENESS

Although bordering and other highlighting techniques really make text stand out, they should be used judiciously. The form of programs should reflect their content; don't be overly clever to the detriment of your program. It is not appropriate, for instance, to use a lot of frilliness in a basically serious program. We believe that proper form and proper function are inextricably interwoven. When they are used well communication is enhanced, but when they are used poorly the message can get hopelessly lost. If you've written a program that people will use frequently, remember that what might seem clever or "cute" the first time through may become extremely irritating after a very short while.

Flash

For example, our Apple has a function called FLASH. When it is invoked, all text following it will "flash" between normal and inverse video. That is, the text will first appear in white letters on a black background, then after about one-half second the same text will appear in the same place except in black letters on a white background, then back to white on black and so on. When used sparingly, such as in "WARNING" messages, the FLASH command can be a real attribute to a program. But many programmers use it with such cavalier abandon that, far from being effective, it becomes incredibly distracting—not to mention hard on the eyes.

WORKING WITH TEXT

Under the best of circumstances using an excellent made-for-computer monitor, reading text from a CRT is fairly easy on the eyes (although it takes some getting used to). But many people who use home computers have their beasts hooked up to TV sets. And text on TV sets is really hard to read (especially apparent when you consider how hard TV is on the brain).

Broken Words

Consider the following output to a computer screen:

```
                    INSTRUCTIONS

WORLD POWER is a game for any number of players. Object of the
game is to control the planet's energy sources through the use of th
reatened nuclear force. The game ends when either one combine co
ntrols all the energy resources of the planet, or when any area exte
nding in a radius of 1000 miles around a combine headquarters ar
e brightly glowing. If the FAMINE light comes on during play, the
combine whose turn it is must decide which POPULATION CENTE
R is to die from lack of food. If the DOOMSDAY sign comes on, all pl
ayers lose...
```

While the game seems interesting, it will be tedious, insulting, and irritating indeed to read extensive directions with many of the lines ending in words sliced down the middle!

We could avoid the broken words by manually counting each character as we typed it into a PRINT statement. As we approached the maximum characters allowed per line we could end the statement and start another one so that no words were ever split up on the screen. We could also use hyphens and split words "naturally"—that is, in between syllables.

But that still seems tedious. We'd much rather have the computer do it for us, since that's the kind of stuff computers do so well. What we need is a routine to act as a filter, searching for words split by the right edge of the screen and preventing the splits before they happen.

An *anti-splitword routine* examines each sentence before the computer spits it out onto the screen. If it discovers a word that will be split if it gets printed "as is," it backs up to look for the space before the word and inserts a carriage return. The first word on the next line is the word that would have been split by the right-hand edge of the screen. It continues in this way until all the text has been displayed.

While not especially long for what it does, our anti-splitword code is somewhat complex. First we'll show you what it looks like (and recommend that you enter and run it). Then, because we feel that this particular routine is an extremely important one, we'll do a line-by-line analysis of how it works. If you are not interested in a complete (albeit lengthy) explication of the code, we suggest you skip ahead a couple of pages to the section marked "Plugging It Into Your Programs."

Listing 1.3

```
0   REM  ANTI-SPLITWORD ROUTINE BY DR. SCOT KAMINS
1   REM  PREVENTS WORDS AT THE RIGHT EDGE OF SCREEN FROM BEING BROKEN
2   REM  SET TOTAL SCREEN COLUMNS IN LINE 10
3   REM  WILL ALSO FORMAT TO PRINTERS
4   REM  THIS ROUTINE WORKS FASTEST WHEN PLACED EARLY IN PROGRAM
5   HOME
10 TC = 40
100  READ A$
110  IF A$ = "END" THEN  PRINT TE$: END
120  IF A$ = "PRINT" THEN  PRINT TE$:TE$ = "": PRINT : GOTO 100
130 A$ = TE$ + A$
140 Y = 0
150 TE$ =  LEFT$ (A$,TC - Y)
160  IF  LEN (TE$) =  LEN (A$) THEN  GOTO 100
170  IF  RIGHT$ (TE$,1) = " " THEN  GOTO 200
180 Y = Y + 1
190  GOTO 150
200  PRINT  LEFT$ (TE$,TC - 1)
210 T =  LEN (A$) -  LEN (TE$)
220  IF T = 0 THEN  GOTO 100
230 A$ =  RIGHT$ (A$,T)
```

Listing 1.3 continued

```
240   GOTO 140
30000   DATA  "WORLD POWER IS A GAME FOR ANY NUMBER OF PLAYERS. "
30010   DATA "THE OBJECT OF THE GAME IS TO CONTROLL THE PLANET'S ENERGY
      RESOURCES THROUGH THE USE OF THREATENED NUCLEAR FORCE. "
30020   DATA "THE GAME ENDS WHEN EITHER ONE COMBINE CONTROLS ALL THE ENERGY
       RESOURCES OF THE PLANET, OR WHEN ANY AREA EXTENDING IN A RADIUS OF
      1,000 MILES AROUND A COMBINE HEADQUARTERS IS BRIGHTLY GLOWING. "
30030   DATA "IF THE FAMINE LIGHT COMES ON DURING PLAY, THE COMBINE WHOSE
      TURN IT IS MUST DECIDE WHICH POPULATION CENTER OF AT LEAST 10,000
      PEOPLE IS TO DIE FROM LACK OF FOOD. "
30040   DATA "IF THE DOOMSDAY LIGHT COMES ON, ALL PLAYERS LOSE... "
30050   DATA "END"
```

You can see that we store our text not in PRINT statements but in DATA statements, one sentence at a time. We use one sentence per data statement to insure that we don't exceed the 239 characters per statement limit our particular computer imposes on us (in general, we can count on a sentence not to exceed 239 characters).

Note the extra space following the period at the end of each data statement. Its function will soon become apparent. The last DATA statement is the word "END." The program uses this to signal that there's no more data to read.

The routine has five variables. TC stands for Total Columns, and refers to the number of columns your CRT will display. Our Apple's video is 40 columns by 24 rows, so we set TC to 40 in line 10. If your computer displays 64 or 80 columns, then TC should equal 64 or 80.

The second variable is A$. Its function is to hold the entire contents of one DATA statement, which we make equal to one sentence for the sake of convenience. Line 100 fetches a DATA statement.

Lines 110–140 require patience the first time you read them. Actually these lines don't come into play the first time the data is "filtered" through, and it isn't until the looping begins in line 160 that this code is really used.

```
110  IF A$ = "END" THEN PRINT TE$ : END
```

Line 110 checks to see if the sentence just picked up by A$ is the signal that the DATA file is empty. It isn't, so the program continues.

```
120  IF A$ = "PRINT" THEN PRINT
     TE$ : TE$ = "" : PRINT : GOTO 100
```

Line 120 introduces TE$, the third variable. It is the temporary storage string that we use in conjunction with A$ to manipulate the data. It will be used to do the actual screen displays, and we'll have more to say about it in a few moments. The line checks to see if the DATA statement picked up by A$ was the word "PRINT." We use "PRINT" as a code word to indicate we want a new paragraph on the screen (displayed as a blank line between blocks of text). If you had entered a DATA statement that was just the word "PRINT," then the contents of the buffer TE$ would be printed followed by a blank line. The program would branch back to line 100 to pick up another DATA statement. TE$ is set to a null string to avoid its contents being printed a second time.

```
130  A$ = TE$ + A$
```

Line 130 really can't be totally understood until the next few lines of code are grasped. But just to give you a frame of reference, this line concatenates (that is, adds together to form a new string) any characters left in the buffer TE$ with the new data picked up by A$. We do that to make sure that no characters get lost in the shuffle.

```
140  Y = 0
```

Line 140 initializes the fourth variable, Y. This variable is used as a "backspacer"—you'll see what that means in a few lines.

```
150  TE$ = LEFT$ (A$, TC - Y)
```

Things will start making more sense from here on out. TE$ gets its initial value here in line 150. Assuming your display is 40 columns wide (TC = 40), the first time this line is executed TE$ is set to hold the first 40 characters of A$.

```
160  IF LEN (TE$) = LEN (A$) THEN GOTO 100
```

In order for us to test for "broken words" between displayed lines we need to have some extra characters in A$ that aren't in TE$. So line 160 checks to see if this is the case. If it isn't, the code goes back to line 100 to pick up another bunch of characters. Let's assume that the code now has enough characters and is ready to go on.

```
170  IF RIGHT$ (TE$,1) = " " THEN GOTO 200
```

Here comes the nitty-gritty; line 170 looks at the last character in the buffer to see if it's a space. The line looks at the TC-characters-long buffer, TE$, and NOT at A$. If the last character *is* a space, which indicates that it *cannot* be in the middle of a word (words do not have spaces in them), then the code branches to line 200 and dumps the buffer onto the screen.

```
180  Y = Y + 1
190  GOTO 150
```

If the last character *is not* a space, then the code advances to line 180, which increments the "backspacer." Then the code bends back to 150, where TC − Y characters, or one less than before, are taken from A$ and loaded into the buffer. The buffer is checked again for the last character, and so on. This process will continue until a space is finally encountered and the program can leave the loop (lines 150–190).

```
200  PRINT LEFT$ (TE$, TC - 1)
```

As we said earlier, line 200 prints TC characters of the buffer. Actually, it prints TC − 1 characters to avoid getting an extra carriage return. The code issues a carriage return—the automatic one implied in the BASIC's PRINT statement. Most terminals issue their own carriage return after the TC'th character is sent to the screen. To avoid this duplication, which would mess up our careful formatting, we don't print the last character. It's just a space and it won't be noticed at the right edge of the screen.

```
210  T = LEN (A$) - LEN (TE$)
220  IF T = 0 THEN GOTO 100
230  A$ = RIGHT$ (A$, T)
240  GOTO 140
```

The last variable, T, is introduced in line 210. Its function is a temporary one, and it is used merely as a flag. If A$ has more characters than TE$ (making T have a value greater than zero), then the unused characters from A$ are put into TE$ (line 230) and the program branches back to line 140 for further processing. If all the characters have been displayed by the time line 220 is reached (in which case T would equal zero), then the code sends us back to line 100 to get more data. Phew! Got all that?

Plugging It Into Your Programs

The entire code can be used as it stands in your programs by setting TC to the proper number, putting the code in a subroutine by changing the END command in line 110 to a RETURN command, and passing the strings to be formatted to the routine as A$. Naturally, you can change the names of the variables to whatever suits you or the demands of your system.

Paging

So now we have our text nicely displayed on the screen and the reader has no problem understanding the information we want to convey. Unless, of course, we have more than a screenful of text! Enter the following code into your beast and RUN it:

```
 5 HOME : REM CLEAR SCREEN
10 FOR X = 1 TO 100
20 PRINT "THIS IS LINE #";X;" FOR YOU TO READ."
30 NEXT X
40 END
```

It should look like this, except in motion:

...and so on until line #100. The problem is that the information just keeps on coming! You'd have to read at computer speed, as opposed to person speed, to keep up. We can't assume that our users are speedreaders, so we need to slow things down for them.

Some computers have a SPEED= function which allows the programmer control over how quickly characters will appear. But that solution introduces another problem since now we need to make assumptions about how fast the user can read. The range of education levels of people using microcomputers in schools and homes goes from the barely literate to the post-doctoral. Unless you know exactly who your users will be, you're in trouble. Those who read faster than what you've estimated will get bored waiting for the computer while those who read slower will get lost and quickly lose interest. So much for effectiveness!

It seems better to let the reader set the speed by displaying text a screenful at a time, stopping the display, and letting the user decide with the press of a key when the next "page" (that is, a full screen) of text should appear.

Here's that runaway program we just saw with a paging routine (called SCREENPAUSE) written around it.

Listing 1.4

```
0   REM PROGRAM TO DEMONSTRATE SCREENPAUSE
1   REM PRESENTS TEXTUAL MATERIAL ONE SCREENPAGE
    AT A TIME
2   REM SET MAXIMUM NUMBER OF LINES/PAGE
    TO BE DISPLAYED AT LINE 25
5   HOME : REM CLEAR THE SCREEN
10   FOR X = 1 TO 100
20   PRINT "THIS IS LINE #";X;" FOR YOU TO READ."
24  COUNT = COUNT + 1: REM INCREMENT LINE COUNTER
25   IF COUNT = 21 THEN  GOSUB 100:
     REM 21 LINES DISPLAYED?
30   NEXT X
40   END
100   REM SCREENPAUSE ROUTINE
110  COUNT = 0: REM  REINIT LINE COUNT FOR NEW SCREEN
120   VTAB 23: REM CURSOR TO VERTICAL TAB POSITION 23
130   INPUT "PRESS THE RETURN KEY FOR MORE...";
      STALL$: REM PROMPT
140   HOME : REM CLEAR THE SCREEN
150   RETURN : REM GET ANOTHER SCREEN OF TEXT
```

Line 24 counts the lines that get printed to the screen. Line 25 checks to see if 21 lines have been displayed. We choose 21 because our CRT displays up to 24 lines at a time, and we want to leave some space at the bottom for a message we'll soon show. If 21 lines have been shown, then the program branches to the subroutine at line 100.

The subroutine at 100 resets the "counter" to zero (so that we can display more pages of text) and prints a message at the bottom of the page alerting the user to press an appropriate key when he or she is ready to see more text. The INPUT statement at line 130 is there just to make the computer wait for the user! It's a "throwaway" since we don't really care what value ends up in STALL$. We're interested only in seeing that the RETURN key gets pressed in the user's own time.

It doesn't take much code to provide great convenience for your users—a total of eight lines, including a REM statement and a RETURN!

To adapt this code to any program that prints text a line at a time, merely place lines 24 and 25 immediately following the PRINT statement, and add the subroutine (lines 100–150 in our example) wherever is convenient.

If you are using a PRINT routine that is likely to be sending more than a line's worth of characters to the screen at any given time, then a modification is in order. Some computers (the Apple II among them) keep a systems variable holding the vertical position of the cursor. In our computer that variable is located at absolute memory location 37. Thus if we say

```
COUNT = PEEK (37)
```

our computer will return the row number of the cursor to the variable COUNT. Substituting that code for line 24 and changing line 25 to read

```
25  IF COUNT => 20 THEN GOSUB 100
```

we still end up with our text nicely "paged" and within the user's control. We'll leave it to you to combine this paging technique with the anti-splitword code we gave you earlier.

FORMATTING NUMBERS

Earlier in this chapter we talked about the difficulty of dealing with text thrown on the screen like a tossed salad of verbiage. What we said about words also goes for numbers. Columns of numbers have their own demands for order. For instance, columns of numbers are easier to understand when their decimal points line up, whole numbers are easier to read when their terminal digits (last ones on the right) are aligned, and so on.

Some BASICs have a wonderful feature called PRINT USING. Among other things, this feature lets the programmer line up decimal numbers through the use of a simple command sequence. Assume that we want to print out five decimal numbers of various length:

```
435.344
12.334443
76889.3
1.77667877678
3.141592675
```

Also assume that we want the decimals to line up:

```
  435.344
   12.334443
76889.3
    1.77667877678
    3.141592675
```

The PRINT USING statement handles this sort of thing nicely. Not all varieties of BASIC have this feature, however. Here's a routine to add to your math-oriented (or dollar-and-cents-oriented) programs to justify numbers around a decimal point.

First, we need to decide in what column the decimal will be. We can choose any place along the horizontal plane of our CRT, just so long as there are enough spaces to the right of that point to accomodate the largest decimal number that we'll use (but see "Overflow" below). We'll arbitrarily pick 22 and assign it to the variable FP (for Fixed Point). Since this will be a constant, we'll define it early in the program:

```
 0  REM PROGRAM TO JUSTIFY NUMBERS AROUND A
    GIVEN COLUMN
 5  HOME : REM CLEAR THE SCREEN
10  FP = 22
```

Note that we usually begin a program with a REM statement in line 0 and a clear screen, the function of line 5. Now we'll initialize a variable called PL (for Points to the Left of the decimal—we'll assign a "real" value to it later) and, after adding an END statement to prevent accidental crashes, construct the first line of the subroutine:

```
 99  END
100  REM DECIMAL JUSTIFICATION SUBROUTINE
105  PL = 0
```

Next we'll set up a loop to look at each character in the number we're dealing with (called NUMBER$ when it's passed to this subroutine—and all the numbers to be "lined up" will pass through this routine, one at a time), searching for the decimal:

```
120  FOR X = 1 TO LEN (NUMBER$)
130  IF MID$ (NUMBER$, X, 1) = "." THEN PL = X - 1
140  NEXT X
```

You'll notice that rather than using real variables (a data type especially set up to handle decimal numbers) we use strings. We do that because our program depends upon the LEN and MID$ functions, both of which work only on string variables. We get our numbers to look like strings to the computer by inputting them as strings, while in an actual application, you would change the number to a string by using Microsoft BASIC's STR$ function. To convert a number called by the real variable name NUMBER to a string variable called NUMBER$, enter the statement

```
NUMBER$ = STR$ (NUMBER).
```

Here's how the program works: let's say the number is 123.4567. The loop is executed four times (i.e., X = 4) before the decimal is found. That means that there are three numbers to the left of the decimal, the decimal being the fourth character in the string:

```
160  HTAB FP - PL
```

Next we tab over to the fixed point for the decimal (established in line 10) and back up as many places to the left as is needed before we

```
170  PRINT NUMBER$
```

and

```
180  RETURN
```

And all the numbers passed to the routine will be lined up around decimals at the FP position. Here's a listing of the code to this point:

Listing 1.5

```
0   REM PROGRAM TO JUSTIFY NUMBERS
    AROUND A GIVEN COLUMN
5   HOME : REM CLEAR THE SCREEN
10 FP = 22: REM SPECIFY "CENTRAL" COLUMN
```

Listing 1.5 continued

```
99  END
100  REM DECIMAL JUSTIFICATION SUBROUTINE
105 PL = 0
120  FOR X = 1 TO  LEN (NUMBER$):
     REM WHERE'S THE DECIMAL?
130  IF  MID$ (NUMBER$,X,1) = "." THEN PL = X - 1:
     REM GET VALUE FOR PL
140  NEXT X
160  HTAB FP - PL: REM POSITION THE CURSOR
170  PRINT NUMBER$
180  RETURN
```

In its present form, the program can't work since no numbers are being sent down to the subroutine. So we'll add a few "dummy" lines, just for a demo:

Listing 1.6

```
0  REM PROGRAM TO JUSTIFY NUMBERS AROUND
   A GIVEN COLUMN
5  HOME : REM CLEAR THE SCREEN
10 FP = 22: REM SPECIFY "CENTRAL" COLUMN
20  FOR Y = 1 TO 5: REM  DO A LOOP FIVE TIMES
25  INPUT "DECIMAL NUMBER, PLEASE: ";NUMBER$(Y)
30  NEXT Y
35  FOR Y = 1 TO 5: REM  NOW TO FORM THE NUMBERS...
40 NUMBER$ = NUMBER$(Y): REM "PASS" THE VARIABLE...
45  GOSUB 100: REM TO THE SUBROUTINE
    IN THE FORM IT WANTS...
50  NEXT Y: REM ...AND GET THE NEXT VARIABLE.
99  END
100  REM DECIMAL JUSTIFICATION SUBROUTINE
105 PL = 0
120  FOR X = 1 TO  LEN (NUMBER$):
     REM WHERE'S THE DECIMAL?
130  IF  MID$ (NUMBER$,X,1) = "." THEN PL = X - 1:
     REM GET VALUE FOR PL
140  NEXT X
160  HTAB FP - PL: REM POSITION THE CURSOR
170  PRINT NUMBER$
180  RETURN
```

Lines 20–30 get five numbers from the keyboard and store them in the array called NUMBER$ (in our BASIC, arrays of up to 10 elements don't need to be dimensioned—check your manual). Lines 35–50 feed the numbers to the subroutine by taking the array elements, one at a time, and equating them to the variable NUMBER$, the name for the variable the subroutine works with. The subroutine takes each number, performs its magic, and prints it on the screen nicely lined up. Here's a sample run of the program, in case you aren't at your machine (we typed in the numbers after the colons in response to the computer's request):

```
DECIMAL NUMBER, PLEASE: 123.4567
DECIMAL NUMBER, PLEASE: 12.34567
DECIMAL NUMBER, PLEASE: 123.4567
DECIMAL NUMBER, PLEASE: 1234.5678
DECIMAL NUMBER, PLEASE: 12345.67890
                          123.4567
                           12.34567
                          123.4567
                         1234.5678
                        12345.67890
```

But we still need to add a few lines of "special case" code to our program. What if the number has no whole number part? What if it has no decimal at all? To compensate for the first condition we insert this line before the loop:

```
110  IF LEFT$ (NUMBER$, 1) = "." THEN GOTO 160
```

Note that the number doesn't go through the loop at all. If we go through the whole number and find no decimal, then we need to back up the whole length of the number and pretend that there's a decimal at the end:

```
150  IF PL = 0 THEN PL = LEN (NUMBER$)
```

And that covers all incidents. Well, almost all incidents. There's always overflow.

Overflow

If the number of characters to the right of the decimal happens to be more than will fit on the screen, our formatting will be blown to smithereens. We could change FP to some lower number, effectively moving the whole display to the left. But sometimes that won't be desirable.

```
8  TC = 40
```

Assuming that a new variable TC equals the Total Columns available, then TC − FP − 1 will represent the total number of characters we can have in the decimal part of the number without causing a carriage return and without overflowing the available space. Let's set up a new variable called AC for Available Columns. The formula (and the actual program line) is

```
15  AC = TC - FP - 1
```

Assuming that TC and FP are defined beforehand, and also assuming that we can "truncate" the displayed number without violating some need of the user, then we should add:

```
165  IF AC < LEN (NUMBER$) - PL THEN
     NUMBER$ = LEFT$ (NUMBER$, AC)
```

And that will do it. Here's the program in its final form (complete with "dummy" lines 20–50) with some added REMs:

Listing 1.7

```
0  REM PROGRAM TO JUSTIFY NUMBERS AROUND A GIVEN COLUMN
5  HOME : REM CLEAR THE SCREEN
8 TC = 40: REM SPECIFY DISPLAY WIDTH
10 FP = 22: REM SPECIFY "CENTRAL" COLUMN
15 AC = TC - FP - 1: REM AVAILABLE COLUMNS
20  FOR Y = 1 TO 5: REM DO A LOOP FIVE TIMES
25  INPUT "DECIMAL NUMBER, PLEASE: ";NUMBER$(Y)
30  NEXT Y
35  FOR Y = 1 TO 5: REM NOW TO FORM THE NUMBERS...
40 NUMBER$ = NUMBER$(Y): REM "PASS" THE VARIABLE...
45  GOSUB 100: REM TO THE SUBROUTINE IN THE FORM IT WANTS...
50  NEXT Y: REM ...AND GET THE NEXT VARIABLE.
99  END
100  REM DECIMAL JUSTIFICATION SUBROUTINE
105 PL = 0
120  FOR X = 1 TO  LEN (NUMBER$): REM WHERE'S THE DECIMAL?
130  IF  MID$ (NUMBER$,X,1) = "." THEN PL = X - 1: REM GET VALUE FOR PL
140  NEXT X
150  IF PL = 0 THEN PL =  LEN (NUMBER$): REM IF STILL NO VALUE FOR PL THEN
      THERE MUST ME NO DECIMAL!
160  HTAB FP - PL: REM POSITION THE CURSOR
165  IF AC <  LEN (NUMBER$) - PL THEN NUMBER$ =  LEFT$ (NUMBER$,AC): REM
     PROTECTION AGAINST OVERFLOW
170  PRINT NUMBER$
180  RETURN
```

When you add this routine to your programs, you should substitute your own code requirements (including values to be passed to NUMBER$) for lines 20–50.

Regular justification of numbers (straight left and right) can be handled exactly as described above in the text section.

SUMMING UP

The computer screen is the communications medium between the program and the user. Its function is to deliver and to solicit information clearly, concisely, and, we hope, aesthetically. The CRT display is one of the ways that a computer touches people, and people should always be touched with caring.

MAYBE THE BUGS ARE OUT OF THE PROGRAM BY NOW
HELP!

CHAPTER 2:

CRASHPROOFING PROGRAMS

In an ideal world somewhere, all computer users always follow directions on computer screens and their fingers never hit wrong keys. This chapter is for those programmers who know that such a world exists only theoretically.

The average computer user will, in response to requests for specific information, supply data not only irrelevant to the question but, if at all possible, fatal to the program. Our user will type in 256 characters when the program can handle only 255, will type a numeric when only an alpha will do, will press the RETURN or ENTER key without entering other data, will type a six-digit number when a one-character letter is needed, and so on.

> WHENEVER YOU CALL FOR THE USER TO TOUCH THE COMPUTER YOU CAN SAVE YOURSELF A LOT OF GRIEF BY SETTING UP A BUFFER ZONE BETWEEN THE INPUT STATEMENT AND THE CENTRAL PROCESSING UNIT (CPU)

This chapter deals with some of the most common violations and gives suggestions and examples of how to deal with them. We'll cover length violations (too many or too few characters), empty inputs (hitting the RETURN or ENTER key without entering any data), and bad inputs (entering inappropriate characters—like pressing a letter when a number is called for). We'll learn how to anticipate these pitfalls and how to write code to handle them.

We'll tell you why it's always best to use string inputs and numeric inputs, how to avoid leading spaces that can mess up search routines, and how to avoid coder's cramps from writing in all this "protection" code. And we've included some neat little bonus subroutines to help you wow your mom and impress your friends.

LENGTH VIOLATIONS

The Empty Input

One usual source of grief is the "empty" input. The screen prompts for an input and the user immediately presses the RETURN key with *no* preceding character. In most cases, this won't do. If your input variable is a real or integer number (which you probably should not be using anyway, the reason for which will soon become apparent), then your computer will probably put an error message on the screen. At best this messes up your pretty screen formatting; at worst (depending on your version of BASIC) your program goes down in flames. Your user ends up sitting there with no idea how to resume program operation—at least without losing some data. If you are using a string for a variable then your program probably won't crash, but you'll have a null string to contend with as well as a field containing incorrect data (i.e., none). This empty input situation can be handled easily by the program if you know how to write the code.

BASIC provides a simple solution to this problem: the LEN function. LEN tells us how many characters are contained in a string. The following program illustrates what we're talking about. This first section clears the screen and asks the user for a name:

Listing 2.1

```
5  HOME : REM CLEAR THE SCREEN
100  VTAB 10
200  HTAB 1
300  PRINT "NAME: ....................<STOP"
400  VTAB 10
500  HTAB 7
600  INPUT "";IN$
650  REM
680  REM
710  REM
740  REM
999  END
```

VTAB and HTAB are cursor-positioning commands on the Apple II. VTAB means vertical tab with limits of 1 and 24, while HTAB means horizontal tab with limits of 1 and 40. They are used extensively in screen formatting. The empty REM statements are place holders that we'll fill in a few minutes.

Here's what the screen should look like:

If in response to this request for a "name" our user presses RETURN without typing anything else, then the name entered will be "" (called a *null* in computer jargon). While that name takes up very little memory space, we must assume that it's inaccurate and, most likely, an accident. So we reject its entry by adding a new line:

```
610  IF LEN (IN$) = 0 THEN GOTO 100
```

This statement says that if there aren't any characters in the input then go back and try again. It goes back to line 100 and not, as you might expect, to line 600 because we want to show the input prompt consisting of the dots, the word STOP, and so on. The null input is rejected and the user notices only a brief flash as the old prompt string (the word NAME, the dots, and the STOP message) is reprinted out on the display.

Not Enough Characters

We can use the general form of line 610 to deal with more specific problems. Sometimes we want at least N characters in an input, maybe for a code. For our example, suppose that at least eight characters are needed. We would modify the line to read

```
620  IF LEN (IN$) > = 8 THEN GOTO 650
```

and add

```
630  GOSUB 1000  :  REM NOT ENOUGH CHARS
```

Translation: if there are at least eight characters in the string then everything is all right, so branch to the next section. If not, then do the next line which says to go to the subroutine at line 1000. We add this subroutine beginning at line 1000:

```
1000  REM NOT ENOUGH CHARS
1010  PRINT''PLEASE TYPE AT LEAST 8
      CHARACTERS.     ''
1020  RETURN
```

And we add the clincher that sends the program back for the input again:

```
640  GOTO 100
```

The subroutine is necessary so that the user knows why an input has not been accepted. Without this message, the user might type the same fewer-than-eight characters all day and never get anywhere!

Here's a listing to date:

Listing 2.2

```
5  HOME : REM CLEAR THE SCREEN
100  VTAB 10
200  HTAB 1
300  PRINT "NAME: ....................<STOP"
400  VTAB 10
500  HTAB 7
600  INPUT "";IN$
610  IF  LEN (IN$) = 0 THEN  GOTO 100
620  IF  LEN (IN$) =  > 8 THEN  GOTO 650
630  GOSUB 1000: REM NOT ENOUGH CHARACTERS
640  GOTO 100
650  REM
680  REM
710  REM
740  REM
999  END
1000  REM NOT ENOUGH CHARS
1010  PRINT "PLEASE TYPE AT LEAST 8 CHARACTERS
1020  RETURN
```

Too Many Characters

The other side of the not-enough-characters problem is the too-many-characters problem. If we have set up our program to accept fields of up to 20 characters and it suddenly must deal with 25, it most likely will stop working correctly (data fields have strong unions). In the example just used, the careful graphic delimiters in line 300 (the dots indicating available spaces and the "STOP" message) give adequate instruction to the user, but is not enough to protect the program from human error. We need something to make sure the user doesn't violate the maximum character limit we've established, so we use LEN again.

```
650  IF LEN (IN$) < = 20 THEN GOTO 680
660  GOSUB 2000 : REM TOO MANY CHARS
```

Translation: if the input string has no more than 20 characters then branch to the next section. If it does have more then 20 then do the next line.

```
2000  REM TOO MANY CHARS
2010  PRINT ''SORRY—ONLY 20 CHARACTERS PER
      CUSTOMER''
2020  RETURN
```

And, of course, we would add

```
670  GOTO 100
```

in order to have the name inputted again. Here's what your program should look like now:

Listing 2.3

```
0   REM  LENGTH VIOLATIONS DEMO
1   REM REJECTS INPUTS LESS THAN 8 CHARS LONG
2   REM REJECTS INPUTS OVER 20 CHARS LONG
3   REM CAN BE MODIFIED FOR ALL CONTINGENCIES
5   HOME : REM  CLEAR THE SCREEN
100  VTAB 10
200  HTAB 1
300  PRINT "NAME: ....................<STOP"
400  VTAB 10
500  HTAB 7
600  INPUT "";IN$
610  IF  LEN (IN$) = 0 THEN  GOTO 100
620  IF  LEN (IN$) =  > 8 THEN  GOTO 650
630  GOSUB 1000: REM NOT ENOUGH CHARACTERS
640  GOTO 100
650  IF  LEN (IN$) =  < 20 THEN  GOTO 680
660  GOSUB 2000
670  GOTO 100
```

Listing 2.3 continued

```
680  REM
710  REM
740  REM
999  END
1000  REM NOT ENOUGH CHARS
1010  PRINT "PLEASE TYPE AT LEAST 8 CHARACTERS        "
1020  RETURN
2000  REM TOO MANY CHARS
2010  PRINT "SORRY - ONLY 20 CHARACTERS PER CUSTOMER"
2020  RETURN
```

Actually, line 610 is now redundant since line 630 guarantees that there be not just one, but eight characters in the input.

Many variations on this theme are possible, of course. If our needs were for exactly 13 characters, we would say

```
620  IF LEN (IN$) = 13 THEN GOTO NEXTPHRASE
630  PRINT "I NEED EXACTLY 13 CHARACTERS      "
640  GOTO 100
```

where NEXTPHRASE is the line to branch to if everything is all right. Since we're dealing with a precise number, lines after 640 in our example are unnecessary (except, perhaps, for "999 END" depending on your version of BASIC).

We could guard against too few and too many characters at the same time (assuming we needed at least one and not more than 20) with

```
620  IF LEN (IN$) > 1 AND LEN (IN$) < 21 THEN GOTO
     NEXTPHRASE
630  PRINT "I NEED BETWEEN 1 AND 20
     CHARACTERS      "
640  GOTO 100
```

Again, the rest of the statements after line 650 are unnecessary. You'll note that we aren't using a subroutine for our error messages here, although we could have. We present this new method just as a variation you might like to experiment with. Subroutines are really useful if you'll use them several times in the same program; however, the examples given here are good if you're just going to use the messages once.

We here at Interaction Central like responsive computers that give specific messages in response to specific user errors. We wouldn't combine messages like the last example does, but we're fanatics. As long as you let the user know completely and clearly what the error is, you're safe.

THE WRONG CHARACTER

Line 300 of our previous "too-long/too-short input de-crashing" program specifically calls for a name, and names of people usually consist of alphabetics. This is not universally true for names, of course, and particularly in stores and factories the names of many parts and products are in fact often numbers. But let's assume that our example is part of a name-and-address data base (for instance, a collection of club members or a mailing list of some kind). What if the user gets confused and starts typing in an address in the name field? Not an uncommon experience for even the most sophisticated computer user, especially after typing names and addresses all day long. You can prevent this kind of "bad-format error" by adding the following lines to our previous program:

```
 680  IF LEFT$ (IN$, 1) > = "A" AND LEFT$ (IN$,
      1) < = "Z" THEN GOTO 710
 690  GOSUB 3000 : REM WRONG CHARACTER
 700  GOTO 100

3000  REM WRONG CHAR
3010  PRINT "FIRST CHARACTER MUST BE A
      LETTER      "
3020  RETURN
```

This simple code determines if the first character is a letter or if it is a non-letter (number, punctuation, space, etc). The LEFT$ function begins at the leftmost character of IN$ and looks at one character, in this case, "1." The effect of the new code is to say "if the first character entered is not a letter, then reject this input and try again."

A MOMENTARY DIVERSION: ASCII CODE

Actually, line 680 is pretty strange. It says, "If the first character is equal to or greater than an 'A' as well as being equal to or less than a 'Z,' then the input is OK." At first glance, this construction looks both ludicrous and baffling, for how can a letter of the alphabet be "less than" or "greater than" anything?

As it turns out, computers are odd things that see the world in terms of numbers only. Microcomputers see the keyboard world (characters entered from your computer's keyboard) in terms of the American Standard Code for Information Interchange (ASCII). ASCII consists of up to 256 codes, which are numbers from 0 to 255. Different computers use certain aspects of the ASCII code differently, but the relationships and values of certain of the codes are standard.

The universally common parts include the numbers zero through nine (ASCII code 48–57) and the letters A through Z (ASCII code 65–90). The ASCII number 66 is always "B," ASCII 67 is always "C," and so on.

When we say ">= A" we're actually saying "equal to or greater than ASCII number 65." So what we're saying in the new line is "if the first letter of the input falls between the ASCII numbers 65 and 90, then it must be a letter and is therefore acceptable." Virtually all computer manuals have copies of the ASCII chart in them, usually in an appendix. We strongly recommend that you check out your own computer's ASCII.

Number, Puh-leez!

If line 300 had called for an address usually beginning with a number instead of a letter, then we could use the same basic format as line 680, changing the parameter values to reflect zero as the lowest acceptable input and nine as the highest:

```
680  IF LEFT$ (IN$,1) >="0" AND LEFT$
     (IN$,1) <= "9" THEN GOTO NEXTPHRASE
```

It's easy to see we use an application of the ASCII table as a filter or a gate that allows only the desired range of input values to be accepted by the program.

In this example, you'd also change the error message to reflect that what's wanted is a number rather than a letter.

It's easy to include exceptions in the line. Let's say that the address could begin with the word *box*, as in a post office box. Add this code:

```
680  IF LEFT$ (IN$, 3) = "BOX" OR ( LEFT$ (IN$, 1)
     >= "0" AND LEFT$ (IN$, 1) <= "9"  ) THEN
     GOTO NEXTPHRASE
```

This statement first checks the beginning three characters of the input to see if they spell the word box. If they do, then the program branches to whatever lines follow the correction routine, as in the previous examples. If they don't, then the first character is checked to see if it is a number. If it is a number, then the program again branches to NEXTPHRASE. But if the input line conforms to neither of these specifications, then the program loops back to the beginning for another try—after delivering an appropriate message, the code for which you can write on your own. (See lines 680-700 for an example.)

Notice that, except where we check for the presence of the word box, we only check the first character in the field. If we knew that the entire field was to contain only letters or only numbers to conform to the necessary format, then we might put the verifying line in a FOR/NEXT loop. We could then check every character. Here's an example checking for just letters:

```
680  FOR X = 1 TO LEN (IN$)
690  IF MID$ ( IN$, X, 1) < "A" OR MID$ (IN$, X,
     1) > "Z" THEN GOSUB 3000 : GOTO 100
700  NEXT X

                     and

3000 REM BAD CHARACTER
3010 PRINT "SORRY—ALL CHARACTERS MUST BE
     LETTERS. TRY AGAIN PLEASE..."
3020 RETURN
```

In the case of the Apple II computer the lines would have to include some housekeeping function to clear the prematurely-exited FOR/NEXT loop (known as "fornextus interruptus" to the cognoscenti). Something as simple as "X = LEN (IN$): NEXT X:" would do nicely and should be inserted into line 690:

```
690  IF MID$ (IN$, X, 1) < "A" OR MID$ (IN$, X,
     1) > "Z" THEN X = LEN (IN$) : NEXT
     X : GOSUB 3000 : GOTO 100
```

Note that we use MID$ here instead of LEFT$. The LEFT$ function lets us check the first N characters beginning at the left-most character, while MID$ lets us check N characters from any position in the string. Since we want the position to move ahead one character each time through the loop, and since we want to check only on one character, we switch to MID$.

If we change the parameter values by substituting zero for "A" and nine for "Z," then the loop will reject an input that is not all numbers. Naturally, you'll want to change 3010 as well.

Now that we've exorcised bad and wrong input characters from the program and printed nice messages to the user, it's time to get into a bit more detail.

CRASHPROOFING RANGES OF PARAMETERS

Sometimes the entries we want are more specialized. Rather than wanting just numbers or just letters, we want a certain range of numbers or letters. For example, we want the user to type a number between nine and fifteen, perhaps in reponse to the question "How many to order (minimum order of nine, maximum order of 15)?" We use a format similar to the one established earlier in line 680 (except now we'll convert the string to its numeric equivalent) and plug in the proper values:

```
675  IN = VAL (IN$)
680  IF IN < 9 OR IN > 15 THEN GOTO REJECT
```

Line 675 uses the VAL function to change IN$ to IN. That's necessary because we're comparing the values of two numbers (compared in ascending order by decimal value) as opposed to two strings (compared in ASCII order, character-for-character).

The same formats (either string or numeric comparisons, depending on what's more appropriate) can be used for any range of individual characters or strings.

Sometimes we have to deal with especially odd limitiations to numbers we can accept. What if we can accept an order for 9 to 15 items, and 20 to 30 items, but not 16 to 19? What if we can accept any number of items from 10 to 85, but not 27? And what if we want 9 to 15, 17, 21, and 139, but nothing else?

Thanks to the Apple's ability to handle logic statements, we can deal with these kinds of sticky problems. Given the above paramaters, line 680 could read like this:

```
680  IF IN < 9 OR ( IN > 15 AND IN <> 17 AND IN
     <> 21 AND IN <> 139 ) THEN GOTO REJECT
```

This statement combines several logic statements with a set of parentheses in order to get the program to do what we want. Expressed in English, this line says,

> "If the number input by the user is less than nine, or if the number is greater than 15 (except for 17, 21, and 139), then reject it."

Here's how it works. The IF statement is interpreted by the computer to be in two major sections, with the OR statement separating the sections. Section one checks if the number is less than nine. If it is, then the rest of the statement is unimportant and the number will be rejected. But we'll assume that the number is not less than nine. Section two is to the right of OR and is enclosed in parentheses. The parentheses are there to insure that BASIC follows the proper precedence in evaluating the code (see the section in your BASIC manual about precedence).

The code on this side of the OR is more complex. It begins by checking if the number is greater than 15. If it is greater than 15, then the program checks if the number is a 17, 21, or 139—the only numbers acceptable. If all that is true, then the number passes the test and the program continues to the next line. If any of those elements are not true, however, the number will be rejected and the program sent to REJECT for an appropriate message and (we assume) another try.

Combining IF statements with various combinations of AND, OR, and NOT (another logic statement, about which see your oft-referenced BASIC manual) and using parentheses to keep things straight, you can set up code to include and exclude any range of elements and exceptions. Don't be scared off by the apparent complexity of this kind of code. All it takes is practice and the willingness to experiment.

ON USING STRING INPUTS

The observant reader will note that even in those cases where we want a number we use a string input instead. There are two basic reasons for this apparently cavalier use of strings. First, strings are easier to manipulate. LEFT, RIGHT, and MID$ functions don't work on integer and real numbers in BASIC (how annoying!), and these string functions are the most convenient ones in BASIC to use for error trapping. Second, many varieties of BASIC will give a rejection (syntax error—program stops prematurely) if a nonnumeric character is entered when a numeric variable is used to accept an input. A string variable, on the other hand, usually will accept anything. The moral: *Accept all inputs as strings.*

Leading and Trailing Spaces

There is a negative side to this lack of discrimination on the part of string variables. Since they accept whatever is typed, they will accept inadvertent hits of the space bar. The string "gobble" is *not* the same as the string " gobble." When the computer looks at "gobble," the first thing it sees after the quote mark is ASCII 71—what we see as a G. But when it looks at " gobble," the first thing it sees is ASCII 32, the space. That means that the name " Martha Mayno" will *never* be found in a data base searching for "Martha Mayno". Goodness knows we don't want to lose poor

Martha! So we'll add the following lines:

```
710  IF LEFT$ (IN$, 1) <> " " THEN 740
720  IN$ = RIGHT$ (IN$, LEN (IN$) - 1 )
730  GOTO 710
```

This code eliminates leading spaces from a string. It keeps on looping until all leading spaces are gone (just in case more than one got in). You'll also want to check for trailing spaces (since "Martha Mayno " will be lost forever), which can be done using similar code. The only real change is the substituting of BASIC's RIGHT$ function for LEFT$ (which works the same way, except backwards—see your BASIC manual or Mitch Waite's *BASIC Programming Primer,* published by Howard Sams, for details). The following two lines of code are based on the way our BASIC handles the "truth" of IF-THEN statements: if the condition is false the program goes to the next line, as opposed to the next statement. Thus we can write:

```
710  IF LEFT$ (IN$, 1) = " " THEN IN$ = RIGHT$ (IN$,
     LEN (IN$) - 1 ) : GOTO 710
720  IF RIGHT$ (IN$, 1) = " " THEN IN$ = LEFT$ (IN$,
     LEN (IN$) - 1) : GOTO 720
```

We keep on looping in lines 710 and 720 until all leading and trailing spaces are gone, just in case the space bar got hit more than once. You may not be able to use this form; once again, check your manual to be sure.

These new lines are different from the other error checkers we have seen in that they automatically correct the error rather than making the user do it.

Here's the program in one version of its final form:

Listing 2.4

```
0   REM  CRASHPROOF DEMO
1   REM WELL, THEORETICALLY CRASHPROOF.
2   REM
5   HOME : REM CLEAR SCREEN
100  VTAB 10: REM POSITION CURSOR TO 10TH ROW,
200  HTAB 1: REM 1ST COLUMN
300  PRINT "NAME: ....................<STOP"
400  VTAB 10
500  HTAB 7
600  INPUT "";IN$
610  IF  LEN (IN$) = 0 THEN  GOTO 100: REM  HIT RETURN BY MISTAKE
620  IF  LEN (IN$) =  > 8 THEN  GOTO 650: REM GOT AT LEAST 8 CHARACTERS?
```

Listing 2.4 continued

```
630  GOSUB 1000: REM  IF NOT THEN GIVE MESSAGE...
640  GOTO 100: REM  ...AND TRY AGAIN
650  IF  LEN (IN$) =  < 20 THEN  GOTO 680: REM MORE THAN 20 CHARS?
660  GOSUB 2000: REM THAT'S TOO MANY! TELL THE USER...
670  GOTO 100: REM ...AND TRY AGAIN
680  IF  LEFT$ (IN$,1) =  > "A" AND  LEFT$ (IN$,1) =  < "Z" THEN  GOTO 710
     : REM FIRST CHARACTER A LETTER?
690  GOSUB 3000: REM IF NOT, TELL 'EM...
700  GOTO 100: REM ...AND TRY AGAIN
710  IF  LEFT$ (IN$,1) <  > " " THEN 740: REM CHECK FOR LEADING SPACES
720 IN$ =  RIGHT$ (IN$, LEN (IN$) - 1): REM AND GET RID OF THEM.
730  GOTO 710: REM CHECK AGAIN TO MAKE SURE.
740  IF  RIGHT$ (IN$,1) <  > " " THEN 999: REM CHECK FOR TRAILING SPACES
750 IN$ =  LEFT$ (IN$, LEN (IN$) - 1): REM AND GET RID OF THEM.
760  GOTO 740: REM AND RECHECK FOR MORE.
999  END
1000  REM NOT ENOUGH CHARS
1010  PRINT "PLEASE TYPE AT LEAST 8 CHARACTERS       "
1020  RETURN
2000  REM TOO MANY CHARS
2010  PRINT "SORRY - ONLY 20 CHARACTERS PER CUSTOMER"
2020  RETURN
3000  REM  WRONG CHARACTERS
3010  PRINT "FIRST CHARACTER MUST BE A LETTER        "
3020  RETURN
```

Subroutines and Coder's Cramps

"My Goodness, that's an awful lot of code to write just to check a simple input," we hear you say (excellent ears we have here on the West Coast—they come from listening for earthquakes).

But the fact is you need write this code only once—and then use it again and again by putting the various sections in subroutines.

We'll take the lines dealing with minimum input length (lines 620–640, 1000–1020) as an example. All we need to do is substitute a variable for the number in lines 620 and 1010 and assign the value of the variable before we encounter the lines.

```
  10  LOW = 8
 620  IF LEN (IN$) = > LOW THEN GOTO 650
1010  PRINT "PLEASE TYPE AT LEAST "; LOW;
      "CHARACTERS"
```

The code dealing with leading and trailing spaces can itself constitute a subroutine if you make sure that IN$ equates to the input string before branching (just like LOW = 8 in the last example). The same technique works for maximum numbers, minimum numbers, or whatever else is needed for error protection on inputs.

As it turns out, writing "bullet-proof code" doesn't really take all that much extra work or extra memory. Subroutines are the key.

THE NUMERIC MENU: A CRUMMY TYPIST'S BEST FRIEND

To paraphrase an old friend of ours, the program input highways are indeed fraught with marauders. And a route especially vulnerable is the one with crossroads where we ask the user to make a selection from a list of alternatives.

Let's assume that you have written a program that tells the retail prices of all models of five major auto manufacturers—Ford, Chrysler, Chevrolet, Volkswagon, and Packard (we're classicists). Your menu could look like this:

```
                MAJOR AUTOMOBILES

Please type the price list you want to see:

                FORD
                CHRYSLER
                CHEVROLET
                VOLKSWAGEN
                PACKARD

Which one?
```

Our user, an energy-conscious buyer and an especially poor typist, enters "VULKSVAGEN." How do you protect against this menace? The examples we have used so far won't do since the input passes the test. We need a spelling checker! So we all hop into a rented Vulksvagen bus and head for the nearest artificial intelligence lab (MIT in the East, Stanford in the West).

The next simplest way is to have a line in your program like:

```
IF IN$ <> "FORD" OR IN$ <> "CHRYSLER" OR IN$
<> ...
```

You get the idea. This "crunch-it-out" method is tedious at best. And what happens if there are 25 or 30 choices!! (Oh, my aching gosubs!)

Ascending the better-way-to-solve-it stairway to that Ultimate Algorithm, we find the array method. Put all the choices in an array and compare the input to the array elements. The "checker" section would look like this:

```
1000  FOR X = 1 TO CHOICES
1010  IF CHOICE$(X) = IN$ THEN GOTO 1040
1020  NEXT X

1030  GOTO REJECT

1040  X = CHOICES
1050  NEXT X
1060  GOTO FOUNDIT
```

Here's an explanation. CHOICES equals the total number of lines and CHOICE$ (X) is the name of the array element being compared to the automobile name typed in. If the program can't find the name, it goes to the REJECT routine, explains to the user where he or she has erred, and seeks another automobile name from the user. If the name entered is OK then the program goes to FOUNDIT. Making the control value X equal CHOICES and saying "NEXT X" in the routine at 1040 is a semi-required housekeeping task in our Apple that pops the FOR/NEXT stack, but your computer might not need it.

Inelegant and klutzy though it may be, this certainly works better than the previous method in that the program won't get fouled up by the bad input. But the user is still left with a lousy typing problem and may end up keying in a choice four or five times before getting it right!

A good way out is to reduce the *quantity* of typing that needs to be done.

> The Axiom of Minimum Contact states that the fewer keys the user must press, the less the likelihood of an error. In the above examples we can reduce the likelihood of error by asking the user to type in a number instead of an entire name.

Our screen will look like this:

```
                    MAJOR AUTOMOBILES

Please type the number of the line you want to see:

                    1) FORD
                    2) CHRYSLER
                    3) CHEVROLET
                    4) VOLKSWAGEN
                    5) PACKARD


Which number?
```

Now all we have to check for is the validity of the number. We, of course, apply our earlier wisdom of using a string to hold our number:

```
IF IN$ <"1" OR IN$ > "5" THEN GOTO REJECT
```

Here's what the whole program would look like, exclusive of the subroutines containing the model and price information (references to which you would insert at line 210):

Listing 2.5

```
10  REM AUTO PRICING PROGRAM
20  REM RUNS ON APPLE II
30  REM LINES 40, 60, 160, 170 ARE SCREEN FORMAT COMMANDS
40  HOME
50 I$ = "MAJOR AUTOMOBILES"
60  HTAB 21 -  LEN (I$) / 2: REM CENTERING ROUTINE
70  PRINT I$
80  PRINT : PRINT
90  PRINT "PLEASE TYPE THE NUMBER OF THE LINE YOU  WANT TO SEE: "
100  PRINT : PRINT
110  FOR X = 1 TO 5: REM AUTO NAMES PRINTED HERE
115  READ CHOICE$(X)
120  PRINT  TAB( 10)X;") ";CHOICE$(X)
130  PRINT
140  NEXT X
150  PRINT
160  VTAB 22
170  HTAB 5
180  INPUT "WHICH NUMBER? ";IN$
190  IF IN$ < "1" OR IN$ > "5" THEN  GOSUB 1000: GOTO 160: REM  CHECK FOR
     "OUT OF BOUNDS" NUMBER
200 CHOICE =  VAL (CHOICE$)
210  ON CHOICE GOSUB N1,N2...NN: REM  DIRECTORY TO PROPER SUBROUTINE FOR
     SELECTED PRICE LIST
999  END
1000  REM WRONG CHOICE
1010  PRINT "NOT ON MY LIST.  NUMBERS 1 - 5 ONLY."
1020  RETURN
2000  DATA FORD,CHRYSLER,CHEVROLET,VOLKSWAGEN,PACKARD
```

VALEDICTORY

There are other input errors that users can make, of course. They can hit the RESET key or elbow the POWER switch or kick out the plug. All we can do is protect against the errors we know and constantly strive to devise more careful, user-proof code. It's either that or go back to CB radios.

I DON'T MIND THAT SHE'S OLD FASHIONED... BUT SHE COULD A LEAST BE A LITTLE FRIENDLIER
PRINT "RIGHT ON"
LOGO
BASIC
FORTRAN

CHAPTER 3:

VERIFICATIONS AND VALIDATIONS

In the last chapter we covered bad inputs from the computer's point of view, when the user enters invalid data that would affect the computer's processing. In this chapter we'll look at input mistakes from the user's point of view, when the user enters untrue data. We'll discuss the errors that users can correct on their own as well as the ones the program should help them correct. We'll also talk about helping computer users correct the errors they thought they had already taken care of.

More specifically, we'll look at ways to minimize user errors, which means, in many cases, minimizing how much we make the user type at the terminal. We'll consider verifying inputs to make sure the user has typed what was meant, and we'll discuss the single-key input GET statement in menu-driven programs. And we'll include such niceties as getting the computer to help the user correct his or her mistakes, auto-typing, and other pro-human features.

CORRECTING MISTAKES

Consider the following. Our computer user has just purchased a mailing list program written by you to hold a Winter Solstice card list (our user used to send Christmas cards, but her Druid Aunt Mildred converted her). She is seventy-five names into her work. Being somewhat tired by this time, she makes a small error:

```
name: JANE Q. KEYPUNCH

street: SAN FRANCISCO■... <STOP
```

(■ = cursor position)

Our user has typed a city name in the "street" field. Looking at the listing, we find:

Listing 3.1

```
5  HOME : REM CLEAR SCREEN
150  VTAB 5: HTAB 1: REM POSITION CURSOR
      FOR STREET FIELD
160  PRINT "STREET: ";: REM SEMICOLON PREVENTS
      FORM FEED
170  FOR X = 1 TO 20: REM PRINT OUT 20 DOTS AFTER
      "STREET"...
180  PRINT ".";: REM ...SO THAT THE USER
      CAN KNOW HOW MANY...
190  NEXT X: REM ...CHARACTERS CAN BE ENTERED
      IN THE FIELD...
200  PRINT "<STOP";: REM ...WITHOUT VIOLATINGTHE
      ALLOWED NUMBER.
210  HTAB 9: REM REPOSITION CURSOR FOR THE INPUT
220  INPUT "";STREET$: REM  NULL STRING INHIBITS
      "?" IN OUR MACHINE
240  REM WE'LL FILL THIS LINE IN A BIT
290  REM  DITTO
300  VTAB 9: HTAB 3: REM  POSITION CURSOR
      FOR CITY FIELD
310  PRINT "CITY: ";
320  FOR X = 1 TO 20
330  PRINT ".";
340  NEXT X
350  PRINT "<STOP";
360  HTAB 9
370  INPUT "";CITY$
999  END
```

No problem, you say. Most computers have a backspace key—ASCII 8 or CTRL H—that a user can press a few times to get back to the beginning of the line. But if the RETURN or ENTER key has been pressed, then there's trouble:

If the RETURN key is pressed and the user discovers there is still a problem, what can be done? The program might have a "change" section that the user can run later to correct any errors. In fact, it's an excellent idea to have such a module in case mistakes are discovered later or information already entered needs to be updated. But such a solution is inefficient and time-consuming when the error is detected at primary data-entry time. There ought to be a more immediate "Oh, I didn't mean that, I meant this" mode to get the user back on track.

Verifying Inputs

As it turns out, such a mode is easily included in nearly all programs. In action it would look like this:

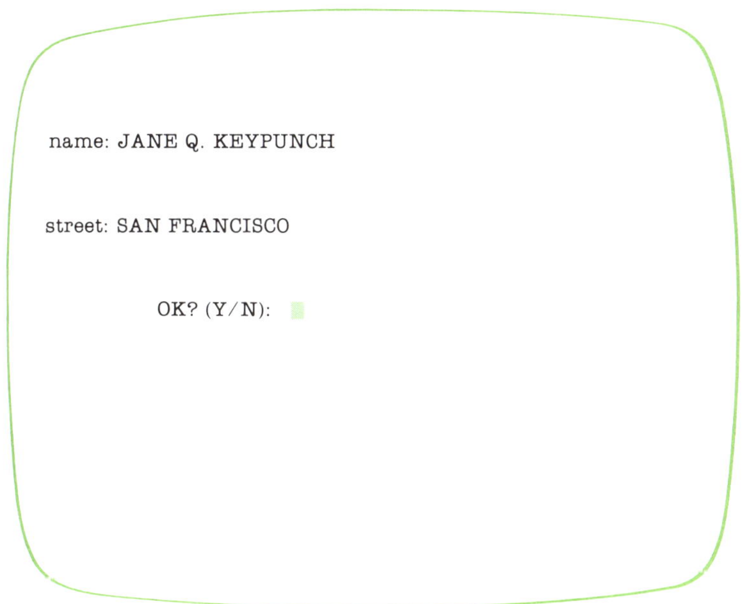

If the user enters "Y," the program accepts the input and moves on to the "city" field. If "N" is typed, then the input is rejected and the cursor is repositioned over the first character in the "street" input field. The user can now type what was meant in the first place. The code is quite simple:

```
230  VTAB 7: HTAB 10
240  PRINT "OK? (Y/N): ";
250  GET QUIZ$  : REM 1—KEYSTROKE INPUT—WE'LL
     EXPLAIN IN A MINUTE
260  VTAB 7: HTAB 10
270  PRINT "                    "
280  IF QUIZ$ = "N" THEN 150
```

Line 230 positions the cursor to print out the question in 240. Line 250 accepts a "Y" for "Yes, you can accept the input just as it has been typed" or an "N" for "No, I made a mistake—give me another chance." Line 260 puts the cursor at the start of the message we displayed at line 240 so that we can erase it by printing blanks over it (which is what line 270 does). We erase it because the message is no longer needed and there is no sense cluttering up the screen with dead messages. Line 280 is the filter line. If the user wants another chance, then the program loops back to the "POSITION CURSOR FOR STREET" code at line 150.

"GET"ing It

Line 250 of the code we just showed you contains a GET statement. Most computers with BASIC have this or an equivalent statement, or one can be worked out. The GET statement accepts one and only one character from the keyboard (it will also accept one character from the disk, by the way). It issues its own RETURN or ENTER without issuing a line-feed or resetting the cursor to the beginning of the line, as in the INPUT statement. It is "non-echoing"—that is, it doesn't print the character it accepts onto the screen (bringing up the idea of passwords for all you security-conscious and paranoid types). Of course, just because you can't see it doesn't mean it's not there. It's like a control character that you only use one keystroke to enter: the computer knows that it's there, even if a human has doubts.

If you *want* to let the user see the character the computer produced from the GET statement, just print it. In the code we just showed you, you could add

```
255  PRINT QUIZ$
```

and the GET character would be displayed on the screen. In this particular case, the code at lines 260 and 270 would wipe it out immediately—it would be printed and erased so fast you couldn't see it! Enter this new line

```
257  FOR STALL = 1 TO 1000: NEXT STALL  :  REM
     DELAY LOOP
```

to slow the computer down a bit and let you see your handiwork.

GET is really useful in those situations where you want to minimize the number of keystrokes the user must enter. The fewer the keystrokes, the less the chance for error.

A Recyclable Checker: Make It a Subroutine

Let's get back to our mailing list. By converting lines 230–280 to a more generalized subroutine, the same routine for getting input can be used throughout the entire program. In such a case you could use the following code instead of lines 230–280 and continue to use the new GET command:

```
240  REM WE'LL NEED THIS LINE SOON
250  V = 7  :  H = 10  :  REM SET VALUES FOR VERT.
     & HOR. CURSOR POSITION
260  GOSUB 1000  :  REM DO THE "OK"ING
270  IF NO = 0 THEN 290  :  REM IF INPUT OK THEN
     DO NEXT SECTION
280  NO = 0  :  REM RESET THE FLAG...
285  GOTO 150  :  REM...AND GET ANOTHER INPUT
```

Now we add the subroutine that will do the work. In reality it's the verifying routine we used in the last example, except this time we use variables rather than constants to keep the code flexible and recyclable:

```
1000  REM OK CHECKER
1010  VTAB V  :  HTAB H  :  REM POSITION CURSOR
1020  PRINT "OK? (Y/N): ";
1030  GET QUIZ$  :  REM ACCEPT 1 CHARACTER AS
      ANSWER
1040  VTAB V  :  HTAB H
1050  PRINT "                    "  :  REM ERASE THE OK
      QUESTION (NO LONGER NEEDED)
1060  IF QUIZ$ = "N" THEN NO = 1  :  REM SET
      "UNACCEPTABLE INPUT" FLAG
1070  RETURN
```

The OK CHECKER subroutine can be used wherever you want to allow the user to verify a single input. Here's a current listing of the mailing list entry program:

Listing 3.2

```
0   REM  MAILER 2
1   REM DEMONSTRATES PRINCIPLE OF INPUT VERIFICATION
5   HOME : REM CLEAR SCREEN
150  VTAB 5: HTAB 1: REM POSITION CURSOR FOR STREET FIELD
160  PRINT "STREET: ";: REM SEMICOLON PREVENTS FORM FEED
170  FOR X = 1 TO 20: REM PRINT OUT 20 DOTS AFTER "STREET"...
180  PRINT ".";: REM ...SO THAT THE USER CAN KNOW HOW MANY...
```

Listing 3.2 continued

```
190   NEXT X: REM ...CHARACTERS CAN BE ENTERED IN THE FIELD...
200   PRINT "<STOP";: REM ...WITHOUT VIOLATINGTHE ALLOWED NUMBER.
210   HTAB 9: REM REPOSITION CURSOR FOR THE INPUT
220   INPUT "";STREET$: REM  NULL STRING INHIBITS "?" IN OUR MACHINE
240   REM WE'LL NEED THIS LINE SOON
250 V = 7:H = 10: REM SET VALUES FOR VERT. & HOR. CURSOR POSITION
260   GOSUB 1000: REM DO THE "OK"ING
270   IF NO = 0 THEN 290: REM IF INPUT OK THEN DO NEXT SECTION
280 NO = 0: REM  RESET THE FLAG...
285   GOTO 150: REM ...AND GET ANOTHER INPUT
290   REM  DITTO
300   VTAB 9: HTAB 3: REM  POSITION CURSOR FOR CITY FIELD
310   PRINT "CITY: ";
320   FOR X = 1 TO 20
330   PRINT ".";
340   NEXT X
350   PRINT "<STOP";
360   HTAB 9
370   INPUT "";CITY$
999   END
1000   REM OK CHECKER
1010   VTAB V: HTAB H: REM POSITION CURSOR
1020   PRINT "OK? (Y/N): ";
1030   GET QUIZ$: REM  ACCEPT 1 CHARACTER AS ANSWER
1040   VTAB V: HTAB H
1050   PRINT "                    ": REM  ERASE THE OK QUESTION (NO LONGER NEEDED
     )
1060   IF QUIZ$ = "N" THEN NO = 1: REM SET "UNACCEPTABLE INPUT" FLAG
1070   RETURN
```

Correction Options for the User

As it turns out, there are several ways of handling this "mistake reentry" business, depending on how nice you want to be to your user. When we reposition the cursor to accept the corrected input in the above example, we automatically erase the old input. But what if the error is a spelling mistake, and all the user wants to change is, say, the fifth letter? How about if the user presses N to signal a change in the input, but discovers (after the cursor is repositioned) that it was right the first time? It seems a shame to have to type the whole line again when it could be automatically done by the computer. The screen would look like this:

Auto-Entry: Let Your Computer Do the Typing

Here's some code that will hand over the task of retyping the line to the computer. It goes with the mailing list example we've been using. First we set up a string called TEMP$. Its value is set to whatever was entered for the name of the street in line 220. If the user wants a chance to correct the entry for "street," the code still goes back to line 150—but this time the prompt line is displayed on the screen with the "bad" entry still there and the cursor positioned over the first character. As far as the user is concerned, the only thing that happened was that the cursor got repositioned. The user sees the old entry and decides what characters are still OK. The "good" characters can be copied over with the foward arrow (character copy key—control U), and the "bad" characters can be replaced:

```
145  TEMP$ = "" : REM CLEAR A STRING VARIABLE
160  PRINT "Street: "; TEMP$; : REM TEMP$ WILL
     HAVE A VALUE SOON
170  FOR X = 1 TO 20 - LEN (TEMP$) : REM
     REFIGURE CORRECT "LENGTH FORM"
245  TEMP$ = STREET$ : REM WE'LL USE THIS IF WE
     SAY "N" IN LINE 1030
290  TEMP$ = "" : REM CLEAR IT FOR NEXT ROUTINE
```

Here's some detail about how this new code works. If the user decides that the original entry is OK, TEMP$ never gets displayed. The first time the computer comes across line 160, TEMP$ has no value (a null string) since it was cleared in line 145 and won't get set to anything until line 245. But if the user signals that a change is necessary (which would happen in the subroutine that gets referenced in line 260), the program branches back to line 150—this time with TEMP$ holding the "bad" data. When line 160 of our new code is encountered, the prompt line is reprinted along with TEMP$.

Line 120 refigures how many dots (".") are needed to prompt the user about how many characters may be entered. Each dot represents one allowable character. If some of those dots have already been used up, we'd better make sure that we don't confuse the user by signalling that there are more allowable characters than there really are. So we take the original allowable number (20) and subtract the number of characters already used up—the number of characters in TEMP$. The first time through the code, TEMP$ has no value, so the number of dots remains at 20 (that is, 20–0).

Finally, line 290 clears the string by resetting the value of TEMP$ to null so that it will be ready to be used again in the next routine without any old value being held to confuse things.

To allow for the situation in which the original answer was correct, we would allow a "carriage return default" condition. If the ENTER key were pressed with the cursor over the first character in the "bad" entry, then the original entry would be taken as valid. This saves the user the time and trouble of copying the line over. Just add this short section of code:

```
230  IF LEN (STREET$) THEN 240  :  REM IF STREET$
     HAS A NEW VALUE THEN SKIP DOWN
232  STREET$ = TEMP$  :  REM KEEP OLD VALUE IF NO
     NEW VALUE GIVEN
234  VTAB 5  :  HTAB 9  :  REM PUT THE CURSOR BACK
     TO THE INPUT POSITION
236  PRINT TEMP$  :  REM SHOW THE OLD VALUE
```

The code says, "If in response to the input request the user presses the ENTER key without typing in any characters, and if TEMP$ has anything in it, then have the input string equal TEMP$."

Auto-Clearing

If you really wanted to be sexy you could include some option that would let the user enter some seldom-used character to erase the old input from the line. This kind of an option is a helpful gift to the user. In this example we'll use the slash ("/") to mean "erase entry." It costs a few bytes of memory, but what the heck:

```
255  IF STREET$ = "/" THEN GOTO 145 : REM "/" IS
     WHAT TO TYPE TO CLEAR THE LINE
```

This statement sends the program scurrying back to line 145 if the user enters a slash. Line 145 clears the value of TEMP$ and goes on to display the prompt line on the screen. Since TEMP$ has no value, the "blank" prompt line is displayed.

On-Screen Prompts

If you provide options you are obligated to tell the user about them on screen at the time of their availability. It isn't enough just to include them in the printed documentation. Chances are the user will forget over time how to access the options. On-screen reminders should be succinct, inoffensive, and "biodegradable"—the program erases them after use. Assuming you've been following along in your computer and will add the code we're about to show you, this will appear on your screen when you answer "N" to the "OK?" question:

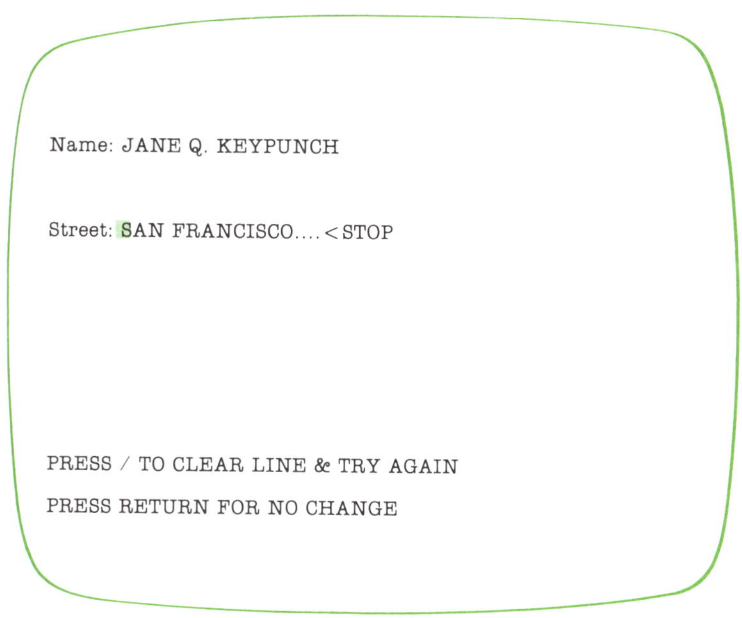

Both screen-bottom "prompting" lines will disappear when the RETURN key is pressed. Here are the additions you'll need to make to the previous code. First for the "carriage return accepts old data" code in lines 270–285, add:

```
283  VTAB 23 : HTAB 1 : REM POSITION CURSOR
284  PRINT "PRESS RETURN FOR NO CHANGE"

240  GOSUB 2000 : REM SCREEN OPTIONS CLEANUP
```

and add this subroutine:

```
2000  REM SCREEN OPTIONS CLEANUP
2010  VTAB 21 : HTAB 1 : REM SET UP CURSOR TO
      CLEAN UP...
2020  PRINT "                                  ": REM
      ...NO-LONGER-MEANINGFUL MESSAGES.

2025  PRINT : REM SKIP A LINE (IT'S BLANK ANYWAY)
2030  PRINT "                                         "
2040  RETURN
```

And for the "slash clears the line" option at line 225, add:

```
225  IF STREET$ <> "/" THEN 230 : REM IF OPTION
     NOT USED THEN BRANCH
227  GOSUB 2000 : REM SCREEN OPTIONS CLEANUP
229  GOTO 145 : REM CLEAR TEMP$ AND TRY AGAIN

281  VTAB 21: HTAB 1
282  PRINT "PRESS / TO CLEAR LINE & TRY AGAIN"
```

Here's what the entire program looks like:

Listing 3.3

```
0   REM "VERIFYING INPUTS" DEMO
1   REM INCLUDES LINE-CLEARING OPTION
2   REM AND "OLD ENTRY OK" OPTION
3   REM
5   HOME : REM CLEAR SCREEN
145 TEMP$ = "": REM CLEAR A STRING VARIABLE
150  VTAB 5: HTAB 1: REM POSITION CURSOR FOR STREET FIELD
160  PRINT "STREET: ";TEMP$;: REM  TEMP$ WILL HAVE A VALUE SOON
170  FOR X = 1 TO 20 -  LEN (TEMP$): REM REFIGURE CORRECT "LENGTH FORM"
180  PRINT ".";: REM ...SO THAT THE USER CAN KNOW HOW MANY...
190  NEXT X: REM ...CHARACTERS CAN BE ENTERED IN THE FIELD...
200  PRINT "<STOP";: REM ...WITHOUT VIOLATINGTHE ALLOWED NUMBER.
210  HTAB 9: REM REPOSITION CURSOR FOR THE INPUT
220  INPUT "";STREET$: REM  NULL STRING INHIBITS "?" IN OUR MACHINE
225  IF STREET$ <  > "/" THEN 230: REM IF OPTION NOT USED THEN BRANCH
227  GOSUB 2000: REM SCREEN OPTIONS CLEANUP
```

Listing 3.3 continued

```
229  GOTO 145: REM CLEAR TEMP$ AND TRY AGAIN
230  IF  LEN (STREET$) THEN 240: REM IF STREET$ HAS A NEW VALUE THEN SKIP
     DOWN
232 STREET$ = TEMP$: REM KEEP OLD VALUE IF NO NEW VALUE GIVEN
234  VTAB 5: HTAB 9: REM PUT THE CURSOR BACK TO THE INPUT POSITION
236  PRINT TEMP$: REM SHOW THE OLD VALUE
240  GOSUB 2000: REM SCREEN OPTIONS CLEANUP
245 TEMP$ = STREET$: REM  WE'LL USE THIS IF WE SAY "N" IN LINE 1030
250 V = 7:H = 10: REM SET VALUES FOR VERT. & HOR. CURSOR POSITION
260  GOSUB 1000: REM DO THE "OK"ING
270  IF NO = 0 THEN 290: REM IF INPUT OK THEN DO NEXT SECTION
280 NO = 0: REM  RESET THE FLAG...
281  VTAB 21: HTAB 1
282  PRINT "/ CLEARS THE LINE"
283  VTAB 23: HTAB 1: REM POSITION CURSOR
284  PRINT "CARRIAGE RETURN = NO CHANGE"
285  GOTO 150: REM ...AND GET ANOTHER INPUT
290 TEMP$ = "": REM CLEAR IT FOR THE NEXT ROUTINE
300  VTAB 9: HTAB 3: REM  POSITION CURSOR FOR CITY FIELD
310  PRINT "CITY: ";
320  FOR X = 1 TO 20
330  PRINT ".";
340  NEXT X
350  PRINT "<STOP";
360  HTAB 9
370  INPUT "";CITY$
999  END
1000  REM OK CHECKER
1010  VTAB V: HTAB H: REM POSITION CURSOR
1020  PRINT "OK? (Y/N): ";
1030  GET QUIZ$: REM  ACCEPT 1 CHARACTER AS ANSWER
1040  VTAB V: HTAB H
1050  PRINT "                    ": REM  ERASE THE OK QUESTION (NO LONGER NEEDED
     )
1060  IF QUIZ$ = "N" THEN NO = 1: REM SET "UNACCEPTABLE INPUT" FLAG
1070  RETURN
2000  REM SCREEN OPTIONS CLEANUP
2010  VTAB 21: HTAB 1: REM SET UP CURSOR TO CLEAN UP...
2020  PRINT "                                                  ": REM ...NO LONGER ME
     ANINGFUL MESSAGES.
2025  PRINT : REM SKIP A LINE
2030  PRINT "                                                  "
2040  RETURN
```

It's hard to know the difference between providing helpful options and becoming excessively frilly. The options that we choose to use are based on our own experiences, both positive and negative. Let your own experience be your guide.

OK CHECKERS

So much for the lightweight stuff. Sometimes a user doesn't know about mess-ups until after having entered a whole bunch of data. In the mailing list example we've been using, for instance, the user might mix up one person's name with another person's street address and not realize it until entering the zip code. It would be really nice if there were a "this whole sequence is OK" checker that happens after all the individual checkers have taken place.

Of course, users may later discover that they still messed up, but we'll deal with that subject later.

Verifying Previously Entered Data

We spoke earlier in this chapter of how nice it would be to have an option that would let a user change data already entered and confirmed as OK. People *do* change their minds, and bad data *will* slip through. This section will show you how to give your users the luxury of, once again, being forgiven for their inconsistencies.

(Please clear the memory in your computer now, since the following examples don't use the code from the previous program.)

To begin, we'll create a name-and-address file that's already full (that is, the name, street, city, state, and zip have already been filled in). We'll assume that your nifty mailing address program, far improved with compact code and subroutines since last we saw it, has stored the name and address of the card for each person on your list in a string array called BUDDY$ (X,Y). We'll make X the number of this particular BUDDY "file," and in this case X will be equal to eight. Each Y element corresponds sequentially to name, street, city, state, and zip code.

NOTE: The data input to an actual program wouldn't have line numbers, of course. Nor do we recommend this example as any way to write a data-base program. In actuality, you'd probably store this data to the disk until you needed it. We do it this way only so that a sample entry can be acted upon by this sample program. Enough of disclaimers and on to the code!

```
18000  REM SAMPLE ENTRY
18005  X = 8 : REM WE JOIN THE PROGRAM-IN-
       PROGRESS AT THE EIGHTH "SET"
18008  REM THE FOLLOWING STATEMENTS
       (18010-18050) INITIALIZE ARRAY ELEMENTS
18010  BUDDY$ (X,1) = "JOHN SCRIBBLEMONGER"
18020  BUDDY$ (X,2) = "253 DATA BUSS WAY"
18030  BUDDY$ (X,3) = "ROMSTOWN"
18040  BUDDY$ (X,4) = "CALIFORNIA"
18050  BUDDY$ (X,5) = "99999"
18060  RETURN
```

Our final assumption is that the user has just entered the zip code and has said "Y" in response to the computer's "OK? (Y/N): "

As luck would have it, a gust of wind blew through an open window as our user was entering the street address and, unbeknownst to the busy typist, pushed a slip of paper with some other address over Scribblemonger's. Buddy Scribblemonger actually lives in San Francisco, miles and miles from Romstown!

We'll pick up the program at that point:

```
100  GOSUB 18000  :  REM LOAD SAMPLE FILE
800  HOME  :  REM CLEAR SCREEN
810  VTAB 4  :  REM POSITION CURSOR
815  REM DISPLAY THIS WHOLE FILE (NEXT 4 LINES)
820  FOR Y = 1 TO 5
840  PRINT Y; ") "; BUDDY $ (X,Y)
850  PRINT
860  NEXT Y

999  END
```

This section shows the file as the user has entered it (in our case, by the sample file at line 18000). Line 840 prints a number followed by a parenthesis and a space followed by the appropriate field. It gets the field from the array loaded by line 805. X was set to eight at line 18005, but in a real program X would be set a counter incremented every time a file is accepted (we define a file as a name-street-city-state-zip code set).

Now comes the part where the user gets the chance to verify or reject the file:

```
870  VTAB 22  :  HTAB 1  :  REM POSITION CURSOR
     FOR MESSAGE
880  PRINT "ANY CHANGES? (Y/N) ";: REM ANOTHER
     CHANCE FOR HUMANITY!
890  GET ANSWER$  :  REM ONLY ONE CHARACTER IS
     REQUIRED
900  IF ANSWER$ <> "Y" THEN GOTO NEXTFILE: REM
     IF EVERYTHING'S OK DO ANOTHER FILE
```

Here's the display of the completed file, allowing the verification step:

```
1) JOHN SCRIBBLEMONGER

2) 253 DATA BUSS WAY

3) ROMSTOWN

4) CA

5) 99999





ANY CHANGES? (Y/N)
```

Of course, our user wants to make a change and therefore enters "Y." The following code tells the computer what to do to handle the change:

```
910  VTAB 22 : HTAB 1 : REM POSITION CURSOR
     FOR MESSAGE
920  PRINT "CHANGE WHICH FIELD (BY NUMBER): ";:
     REM NO NEED TO TYPE WHOLE STRINGS
930  GET ANSWER$ : REM JUST ONE NUMBER
935  IF ANSWER$ <"1" OR ANSWER$ > "5" THEN
     910 : REM IF WHAT'S TYPED IS OUT OF RANGE
     THEN GO FOR ANOTHER INPUT
```

This code gets a number between one and five, corresponding to the field that needs correcting. We display line 920 *over* the old question, effectively erasing what's no longer needed.

If this were like some programs we've seen, the user would be expected to retype the entire file. That, of course, is cruel and unusual punishment. We ask the user to type only that which is necessary. Here's the code for this step:

```
940  Y = VAL (ANSWER$) : REM CONVERT THE
     STRING TO A REAL NUMBER MATCHING THE
     APPROPRIATE ARRAY DIMENSION
950  ON Y GOSUB 10010, 10020, 10030, 10040,
     10050 : REM GO GET SOME PARAMETERS
```

Line 940 uses the variable Y to match the Y coordinate of the two-dimensional array BUDDY$ (X,Y). Since X = 8, we are only concerned with what field we're looking at, which brings us to the subroutine sets beginning at 10000. We'll soon add code that will use these lines:

```
10000  REM PARAMETERS
10010  FIELD$ = "NAME" : LIMIT = 25 : RETURN
10020  FIELD$ = "STREET" : LIMIT = 20 : RETURN
10030  FIELD$ = "CITY" : LIMIT = 20 : RETURN
10040  FIELD$ = "STATE" : LIMIT = 2 : RETURN
10050  FIELD$ = "ZIP CODE" : LIMIT = 5 : RETURN
11000  REM LENGTH FORM
11010  FOR Z = 1 TO LIMIT : REM GOT LIMIT
       SOMEWHERE AROUND LINE 10000
11020  PRINT ".";
11030  NEXT Z
11040  PRINT "<STOP";
11050  HTAB LEN (FIELD$) + 2 : REM REPOSITION
       THE CURSOR ALLOWING FOR NEATNESS
       (WHICH DEFINITELY COUNTS)
11060  RETURN
```

We need values for FIELD$ and LIMIT to determine what will be printed out by the subroutine at line 11000. The values change depending on which field needs changing:

```
960  VTAB 22 : HTAB 1 : REM POSITION CURSOR
     FOR MESSAGE
965  PRINT "                                    ";: HTAB 1
     : REM CLEAR OUT OLD MESSAGE AND
     REPOSITION CURSOR
970  PRINT FIELD$; " ";: GOSUB 11000 : REM SHOW
     THIS FIELD'S "DESIGNATION" AND PRINT OUT
     LENGTH-LIMITING "FORM"
```

So that we don't get lost, here's the current listing:

Listing 3.4

```
100   GOSUB 18000: REM LOAD SAMPLE FILE
800   HOME : REM CLEAR SCREEN
810   VTAB 4: REM POSITION CURSOR
820   FOR Y = 1 TO 5
840   PRINT Y;") ";BUDDY$(X,Y): REM DISPLAY THIS WHOLE FILE
850   PRINT
860   NEXT Y
870   VTAB 22: HTAB 1: REM POSITION CURSOR FOR MESSAGE
880   PRINT "ANY CHANGES? (Y/N) ";: REM YET ANOTHER CHANCE FOR HUMANITY!
890   GET ANSWER$: REM ONLY ONE CHARACTER IS REQUIRED
900   IF ANSWER$ <  > "Y" THEN  GOTO  NEXT FILE: REM IF EVERYTHING'S OK DO
      ANOTHER FILE
910   VTAB 22: HTAB 1: REM POSITION CURSOR FOR MESSAGE
920   PRINT "CHANGE WHICH FIELD (BY NUMBER): ";: REM NO NEED TO TYPE WHOLE
      STRINGS
930   GET ANSWER$: REM JUST ONE NUMBER
935   IF ANSWER$ < "1" OR ANSWER$ > "5" THEN 910: REM IF WHAT'S TYPED IS
      OUT OF RANGE THEN GO FOR ANOTHER INPUT
940 Y =  VAL (ANSWER$): REM  CONVERT THE STRING TO A REAL NUMBER MATCHING
      THE APPROPRIATE ARRAY DIMENSION
950   ON Y GOSUB 10010,10020,10030,10040,10050: REM GO GET SOME PARAMETERS
960   VTAB 22: HTAB 1: REM POSITION CURSOR FOR MESSAGE
970   PRINT FIELD$;" ";: GOSUB 11000: REM   SHOW THIS FIELD'S "DESIGNATION"
      AND PRINT OUT LENGTH - LIMITING "FORM"
999   END
10000  REM PARAMETERS
10010 FIELD$ = "NAME":LIMIT = 25: RETURN
10020 FIELD$ = "STREET":LIMIT = 20: RETURN
10030 FIELD$ = "CITY":LIMIT = 20: RETURN
10040 FIELD$ = "STATE":LIMIT = 2: RETURN
10050 FIELD$ = "ZIP CODE":LIMIT = 5: RETURN
11000  REM LENGTH FORM
11010  FOR Z = 1 TO LIMIT: REM GOT LIMIT SOMEWHERE AROUND LINE 10000
11020  PRINT ".";
11030  NEXT Z
11040  PRINT "<STOP";
11050  HTAB  LEN (FIELD$) + 2: REM REPOSITION THE CURSOR ALLOWING FOR
      NEATNESS (WHICH DEFINITELY COUNTS)
11060  RETURN
18000  REM SAMPLE FILE
18005 X = 8: REM WE JOIN THE PROGRAM IN PROGRESS AT THE EIGTH "SET"
18010 BUDDY$(X,1) = "JOHN SCRIBBLEMONGER"
18020 BUDDY$(X,2) = "253 DATA BUSS WAY"
18030 BUDDY$(X,3) = "ROMSTOWN"
18040 BUDDY$(X,4) = "CA"
18050 BUDDY$(X,5) = "99999"
18060  RETURN
```

The referenced subroutine at line 11000 prints out a kind of prompt-line "form" for the user to fill in, limiting the number of allowable characters in a particular field (the field lengths used, by the way, are arbitrary and used just for examples). This corresponds to the routine we saw in the last example's lines 160–210, made more useful as a subroutine:

Assuming our user wants to change the city field and enters a "3," the screen would look like this.

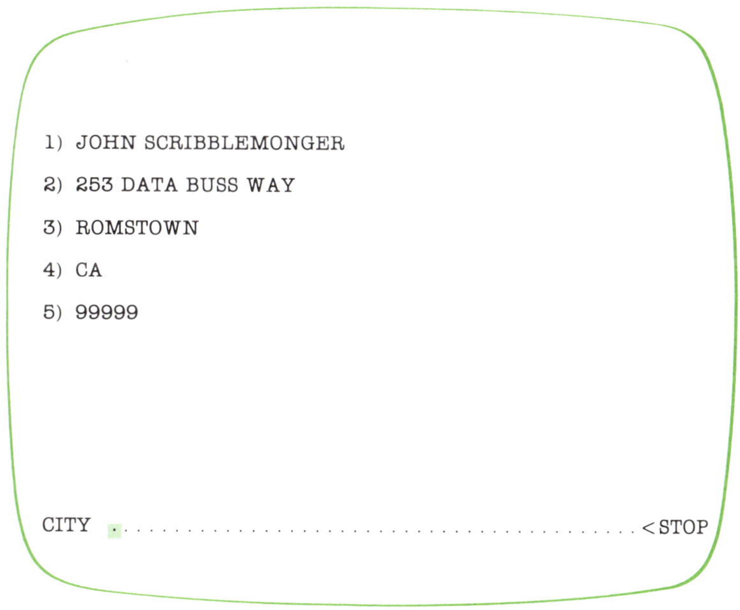

Now we get the actual correction from the user, allowing a null input to default to the original value of the field in question:

```
980  INPUT ""; IN$  :  REM GET THE CORRECTION
985  IF LEN (IN$) = 0 THEN IN$ = BUDDY$
     (X,Y) : REM DEFAULT CARRIAGE RETURN SAYS
     "OLD FIELD WAS OK"
988  BUDDY$ (X,Y) = IN$  :  REM PUT NEW FIELD
     WHERE IT BELONGS
```

This "PRESS RETURN TO ACCEPT OLD DATA" option is especially necessary here since we used a GET command to choose the number of the incorrect field. The GET command operates without the need of the ENTER key—which means it issues a carriage return of its own as soon as a key has been pressed. GET is unforgiving of mistakes in keypresses—you can't backspace if you blow it. And it's really easy to hit a wrong key!

Finally, after the user types in the new information, we send the program back to the beginning of this section to see if everything is, at last, OK:

```
990  GOTO 800 : REM SHOW IT ALL AGAIN FOR
     APPROVAL
999  END
```

There are more prominent ways of displaying this stuff. You could make the changes right on top of the original data rather than at the bottom of the screen, for instance. You could add a "bel" (ASCII code #7) that would issue a beep sound when a user pressed the wrong key (just one "beep"—have pity on the user's ears). You might even consider writing a "spelling checker" that would check for probable errors in name or address entry (a street with eight consonants in a row, for instance). But we'll leave that to your own creativity.

In its final form, here's the "alterations verify" example program:

Listing 3.5

```
0   REM "WHOLE FILE" VERIFYING
1   REM DEMONSTRATES VERIFYING TECHNIQUE
2   REM FOR A NUMBER OF DATA FIELDS
3   REM PREVIOUSLY ENTERED
4   REM
100  GOSUB 18000: REM LOAD SAMPLE FILE
800  HOME : REM CLEAR SCREEN
810  VTAB 4: REM POSITION CURSOR
820  FOR Y = 1 TO 5
840  PRINT Y;") ";BUDDY$(X,Y): REM DISPLAY THIS WHOLE FILE
850  PRINT
860  NEXT Y
870  VTAB 22: HTAB 1: REM POSITION CURSOR FOR MESSAGE
880  PRINT "ANY CHANGES? (Y/N) ";: REM YET ANOTHER CHANCE FOR HUMANITY!
890  GET ANSWER$: REM ONLY ONE CHARACTER IS REQUIRED
900  IF ANSWER$ <  > "Y" THEN  GOTO 999: REM IF EVERYTHING'S OK DO ANOTHER
      FILE
910  VTAB 22: HTAB 1: REM POSITION CURSOR FOR MESSAGE
920  PRINT "CHANGE WHICH FIELD (BY NUMBER): ";: REM NO NEED TO TYPE WHOLE
     STRINGS
930  GET ANSWER$: REM JUST ONE NUMBER
935  IF ANSWER$ < "1" OR ANSWER$ > "5" THEN 910: REM IF WHAT'S TYPED IS
     OUT OF RANGE THEN GO FOR ANOTHER INPUT
940 Y =  VAL (ANSWER$): REM  CONVERT THE STRING TO A REAL NUMBER MATCHING
     THE APPROPRIATE ARRAY DIMENSION
950  ON Y GOSUB 10010,10020,10030,10040,10050: REM GO GET SOME PARAMETERS
960  VTAB 22: HTAB 1: REM POSITION CURSOR FOR MESSAGE
965  PRINT "                                                ";: HTAB 1: REM  CLEAR
     OUT OLD MESSAGE AND REPOSITION CURSOR
970  PRINT FIELD$;" ";: GOSUB 11000: REM   SHOW THIS FIELD'S "DESIGNATION"
     AND PRINT OUT LENGTH - LIMITING "FORM"
980  INPUT "";IN$: REM GET THE CORRECTION
```

Listing 3.5 continued

```
985  IF  LEN (IN$) = 0 THEN IN$ = BUDDY$(X,Y): REM DEFAULT CARRIAGE RETURN
      SAYS "OLD FIELD WAS OK"
988 BUDDY$(X,Y) = IN$: REM PUT NEW FIELD WHERE IT BELONGS
990  GOTO 800: REM SHOW IT ALL AGAIN FOR APPROVAL
999  END
10000  REM PARAMETERS
10010 FIELD$ = "NAME":LIMIT = 25: RETURN
10020 FIELD$ = "STREET":LIMIT = 20: RETURN
10030 FIELD$ = "CITY":LIMIT = 20: RETURN
10040 FIELD$ = "STATE":LIMIT = 2: RETURN
10050 FIELD$ = "ZIP CODE":LIMIT = 5: RETURN
11000  REM LENGTH FORM
11010  FOR Z = 1 TO LIMIT: REM GOT LIMIT SOMEWHERE AROUND LINE 10000
11020  PRINT ".";
11030  NEXT Z
11040  PRINT "<STOP";
11050  HTAB  LEN (FIELD$) + 2: REM REPOSITION THE CURSOR ALLOWING FOR
     NEATNESS (WHICH DEFINITELY COUNTS)
11060  RETURN
18000  REM SAMPLE FILE
18005 X = 8: REM WE JOIN THE PROGRAM IN PROGRESS AT THE EIGTH "SET"
18010 BUDDY$(X,1) = "JOHN SCRIBBLEMONGER"
18020 BUDDY$(X,2) = "253 DATA BUSS WAY"
18030 BUDDY$(X,3) = "ROMSTOWN"
18040 BUDDY$(X,4) = "CA"
18050 BUDDY$(X,5) = "99999"
18060  RETURN
```

RECAP

In this chapter we've dealt with the all-too-human propensity for making mistakes. We've shown that people can err when they enter data for the first time, when they correct their original errors, and, in fact, anytime they touch the keyboard. Best of all, we've shown you how to help people overcome their "finger slips" by writing human-centered code that recognizes and takes into account human fallibility.

1.
TYPE: PRINT
2.
TYPE: OPEN DATA
3.
TYPE: INPUT
4.
TYPE: NAME $
5.
TYPE: PEEK (X)
6.
TYPE: SWAP A, B
7.
TYPE: GOTO CODE
8.
TYPE: RETURN
9.
NOW SAY PLEASE

CHAPTER 4:

DIRECTIONS ON THE DISPLAY

One of the greatest problems with computer programs is that users can't figure out how to use them. Many programs are written with few directions, and some we've seen have no instructions at all. The purpose of this chapter is to aid you in ridding the world of "uninstructioned" programs by showing you how to write programs with directions built into them. We'll give you ideas on how to add directions in both textual and graphic form to the main body of your program, and we'll provide some tips on how to store longish directions out to the disk. And, as usual, we've included some bonus programming tips and algorithms to help make your programming more interactive.

Directions that live in the program (as opposed to directions that live in the hard-copy documentation) should serve to guide the user through the program quickly and clearly. They should be as simple as possible. Let Occam's Razor prevail!

OCCAM'S RAZOR

William of Occam was a fourteenth century English philosopher who liked pithy sayings. Among his pithiest was one which, even today, pithy-saying quoters are wont to quote:

> Entities Should Not Be Multiplied Unnecessarily.

Occam's Razor (as the pithy quoters have named this saying) breaks down to mean the simplest of competing theories is to be preferred and explanations of unknown phenomena are to be sought first in terms of known quantities.

In short, keep it simple. This chapter will show you how.

TEXTUAL MESSAGES

When you must use words to give on-screen directions, be as compact as you can. The detailed information has already been given in the hard-copy documentation (which has its own chapter) or can be had in the help menu (which we'll get to in a bit). The on-screen stuff should be mere reminders.

A Little Addition Program— A Negative Example

Take the case of this little program that tests addition. The program will generate two random numbers for us to add, will tell us if our addition is right or wrong, and will then get another example for us to do.

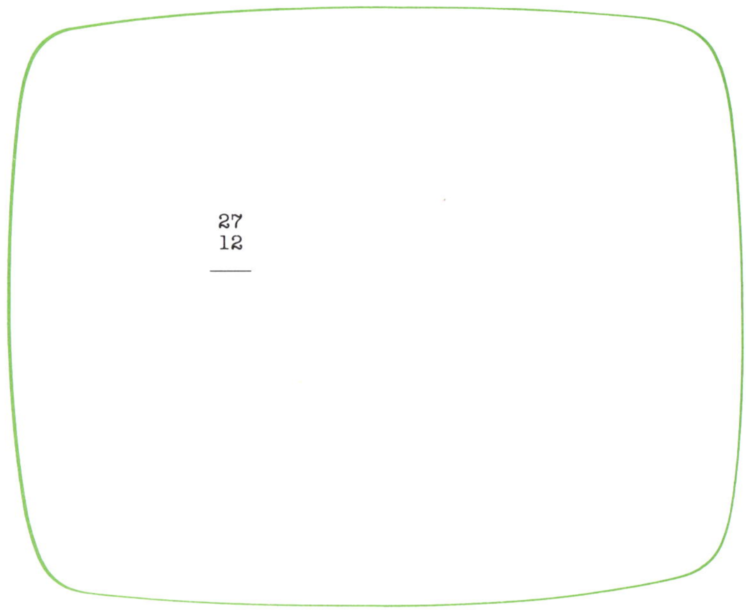

While there are no bugs in this program in the strictest sense, it is non-humanized—it's tough to figure out what to do! Crunch it into your computer and run it. Then we'll work on it together:

Listing 4.1

```
0   HOME : REM CLEAR THE SCREEN
10 N1 =  INT ( RND (1) * 100): REM GET A RANDOM WHOLE # BETWEEN 0 AND 99
20 N2 =  INT ( RND (1) * 100): REM  AND ANOTHER ONE
30 N3 = N2 + N1: REM ADD 'EM UP
40  VTAB 9: HTAB 15: PRINT N1: REM DISPLAY THE FIRST NUMBER NEATLY
50  HTAB 15: PRINT N2: REM PUT THE SECOND NUMBER UNDER THE FIRST
60  HTAB 15: PRINT  CHR$ (95); CHR$ (95): REM UNDERLINE THE COLUMN
80  HTAB 15: INPUT "";AN$: REM ...CAN TYPE IN THE ANSWER
90  VTAB 20: HTAB 13: REM  POSITION CURSOR
100  IF  VAL (AN$) = N3 THEN  PRINT "RIGHT": REM ...OF SUCCESS...
110  IF  VAL (AN$) <  > N3 THEN  PRINT "SORRY. ";N1;" + ";N2;" IS ";N3: REM
     ...OR CONDOLENCE AND CORRECTION.
115  PRINT
120  PRINT "PRESS M FOR MORE";
130  GET A$: REM  ACCEPT A SINGLE CHARACTER FROM THE KEYBOARD.
150  GOTO 0: REM DO IT AGAIN.
```

The two most obvious faults with this program are that the program doesn't tell you what to do or how to stop.

Entrances and Exits

The user might be able to figure out what to do to get things going, but there's not much of a payoff in taking too much for granted. Modify line 80:

```
80  HTAB 10 : INPUT ''SUM: '';AN$
```

In its current state, there's no way for a user to end a session with this program. It doesn't take much code to resolve the problem, however:

```
120  HTAB 10: PRINT ''PRESS M FOR MORE OR E TO
     END'';
140  IF A$ = ''E'' THEN END
```

For some reason many programmers don't think to include exit modes (ways for a user to end a session). No matter how much you're enjoying using a particular program, at some point you're going to want to stop using it for the day. There ought to be an "out," other than the computer's power switch.

Now that we've added an exit option, the directions are more complete. The user knows what to do to get things moving and how to get things stopped. But just to be sure...

Simple On-Screen Instructions

It wouldn't hurt to add more specific instructions to the screen display. First we might tell what to do in words:

```
8  VTAB 1: HTAB 13: PRINT ''ADD THE NUMBERS''
```

Next, we could tell what to do with a symbol:

```
48  HTAB 13: PRINT '' +'';
```

Symbols are compact and clear, while words are often fuzzy and voluminous. We'll have more to say about non-wordy directions in a few pages.

Back with our addition example, it's probably a good idea to change line 80 one more time to make what we want from the user perfectly clear:

```
80 INPUT "THE ANSWER IS ";AN$
```

Finally, for the sake of neatness and to avoid any confusion, we'll provide for reformatting the numbers in case single digits need to be aligned to the right-hand column:

```
42 IF N1 < 10 THEN PRINT " ";
52 IF N2 < 10 THEN PRINT " ";
```

The content of the program is obviously either for kids or for remedial adults (how many physics majors do you know who need practice adding two-digit numbers?). The added directions take into account the audience to whom the program is directed. It might not be obvious to a kid or to a remedial adult student that the problem is addition or that the word "sum" means "the added total." Following through on this theme, we also might change the "end the program" symbol from an E for End to an S for Stop since a kid is more likely to think "I want to stop now" rather than "I want to end" (although there's nothing wrong with setting things up so that both "E" and "S" would stop the program, even if you just advertised the "S").

Here's what the final version will look like on the screen:

```
                      ADD THE NUMBERS




               26
             +  7
               ___
THE ANSWER IS  32




           SORRY. 26 + 7 IS 33

PRESS M FOR MORE OR S TO STOP
```

And here's the listing in its final form:

Listing 4.2

```
0  HOME : REM CLEAR THE SCREEN
5  VTAB 1: HTAB 13: PRINT "ADD THE NUMBERS"
10 N1 =  INT ( RND (1) * 100): REM GET A RANDOM WHOLE # BETWEEN 0 AND 99
20 N2 =  INT ( RND (1) * 100): REM AND ANOTHER ONE
30 N3 = N2 + N1: REM ADD 'EM UP
40  VTAB 9: HTAB 15: IF N1 < 10 THEN  PRINT " ";
43  PRINT N1: REM DISPLAY THE FIRST NUMBER NEATLY
45  HTAB 13: PRINT "+";
50  HTAB 15: IF N2 < 10 THEN  PRINT " ";
55  PRINT N2
60  HTAB 15: PRINT  CHR$ (95); CHR$ (95): REM UNDERLINE THE COLUMN
80  INPUT "THE ANSWER IS ";AN$
90  VTAB 20: HTAB 13: REM POSITION THE CURSOR
100  IF  VAL (AN$) = N3 THEN  PRINT "RIGHT": REM ...OF SUCCESS...
110  IF  VAL (AN$) <  > N3 THEN  PRINT "SORRY. ";N1;" + ";N2;" IS ";N3: REM
     ...OR CONDOLANCE AND CORRECTION.
115  PRINT
120  PRINT "PRESS M FOR MORE OR S TO STOP";
130  GET A$: REM ACCEPT A SINGLE CHARACTER FROM THE KEYBOARD.
140  IF A$ = "S" OR A$ = "E" THEN  END
150  GOTO 0: REM DO IT AGAIN
```

GRAPHIC DIRECTIONS AND CREATIVE PUNCTUATION

One of the pithiest (love that word!) ways to give directions is through the use of graphics. We don't mean you have to be an artist or that your computer must have graphics capabilities. We mean that you can "draw the user a picture" to describe what you mean by the way you format your display.

Tricky Formats: Dates

In our last example, the only entries we called for from the user were numbers. The instructions, therefore, were quite simple. Would that all entries were so simple! Take something as common as a date input. The screen says:

and the program waits for the user to reply. It's clear that the computer wants the user to type in the date, but *how* the date is to be entered isn't even hinted at. The user could reply in at least the following ways:

JULY 4, 1986
7.4.86
7/4/86
4 JULY, 1986
FOURTH OF JULY, '86
JULY THE FOURTH

These are not, of course, the only possible entries that would satisfy the one instruction given—to type in today's date. Unless the input routines are extremely sophisticated, the program will recognize two or three different input forms at best. If the user hasn't been lucky enough to chance upon the necessary format, and if the program doesn't immediately commit hara-kiri (which in the case of such poor human interfacing would indeed be the honorable way out), the user will have to take another stab at what is supposed to be typed.

Much trouble would have been saved had the prompt read:

```
  (EXAMPLE: 05/23/85)
TODAY'S DATE: ../../..
```

First an example of a proper date is given. Without wasting a lot of words, the example demonstrates that two characters are expected for each of three sections, that the three sections should bc separated by slashes, that numbers should be used, and that the proper sequence is month/day/year.

To insure clarity a delineated form is provided for the user, with the cursor appropriately positioned for the first character of his input. The user has a double shot at being right the first time. Here's how to set up a date "form" using BASIC code:

```
 0  HOME
 5  VTAB 5 : HTAB 10 : REM POSITION CURSOR
 6  PRINT "(EXAMPLE: 05/23/85)"
10  PRINT "TODAY'S DATE:       ../../..";: REM 6
    BLANKS
20  HTAB 20 : REM POSITON CURSOR
30  INPUT ""; DTE$ : REM EMPTY QUOTE KEEPS "?"
    FROM APPEARING
```

The directions are clear and concise without wasting a word. William of Occam would have been proud.

Trickier Still: Telephone Numbers

Telephone numbers can be a real pain in the character-input buffer. The ways to mess up a phone entry are myriad. Do you want an area code? Parentheses around them? How about a dash between the prefix and the number? Once again, the simple-to-construct-and-elegant-to-use form is a good solution:

The code for this one is a bit more complex. We don't want the user to have to bother with those pesky dashes between the area code and the prefix and between the prefix and the four-digit number. We'll use the GET statement to handle that problem. First, we'll set up the form:

```
 0  REM PHONE NUMBER DEMO
10  HOME  :  REM CLEAR THE SCREEN
30  COUNT = 0  :  REM INITIALIZE A COUNTER (TO BE
    USED SOON)
35  PHNE$ = ""  :  REM INIT A STRING TO HOLD THE
    PHONE NUMBER
50  VTAB 9  :  HTAB 1  :  REM POSITION CURSOR FOR
    EXAMPLE
55  PRINT "EXAMPLE: 415-555-0000"  :  REM GIVE
    SAMPLE TO FOLLOW
60  HTAB 3  :  REM POSITION CURSOR FOR FORM
65  PRINT"PHONE: ...-...-....";  :  REM NOTE SEMICOLON
    TO PREVENT CR
70  HTAB 10  :  REM POSITION CURSOR FOR INPUT
80  GET NUMBER$  :  REM WAIT FOR A CHARACTER
    FROM THE KEYBOARD
```

So far we have the form displayed and the cursor properly positioned to accept the numbers. The next two lines, 210 and 220, test to see if the last number input came right before a dash—either the third number (the last one in the area code) or the sixth one (the last number in the prefix). If it does, then a space is skipped so that the dashes on the screen are not written over. The count of the numbers already typed comes at line 250:

```
210  IF COUNT = 3 THEN HTAB 11 + COUNT
220  IF COUNT = 6 THEN HTAB 12 + COUNT
230  GET NUMBER$ : REM ACCEPT A NUMBER FROM
     THE KEYBOARD
240  IF NUMBER$ < "0" OR NUMBER$ > "9" THEN
     230 : REM IF CHARACTER ENTERED IS NOT A
     NUMBER THEN TRY AGAIN
250  COUNT = COUNT + 1 : REM INCREMENT COUNT
     OF ACCEPTED CHARACTERS
260  PRINT NUMBER$; : REM DISPLAY THE
     CHARACTER ON SCREEN
270  PHNE$ = PHNE$ + NUMBER$ : REM ADD THIS
     NUMBER TO THE PHONE NUMBER
280  IF COUNT = 10 THEN GOTO 300 : REM IF THAT
     WAS THE LAST NUMBER THEN BRANCH
290  GOTO 210 : REM IF NOT THEN GET ANOTHER
     NUMBER
```

Of course, we want to make sure that the number entered is correct, so we ask the user to verify:

```
300  PRINT : PRINT : INPUT "OK? (Y/N) "; ANSWER$
310  IF LEFT$ (ANSWER$,1) < > "Y" THEN GOTO
     10 : REM IF PHONE NUMBER REJECTED GET A
     NEW ONE
320  REM REST OF PROGRAM GOES HERE
999  END
```

We demand a "yes" answer (or at least the letter "Y") before we accept the phone number as correct. Actually, we prefer to allow a default condition also to mean "yes"—that is, if just the ENTER or RETURN key is pressed we assume the answer is OK. We would change line 310 to read:

```
310  IF LEFT$ (ANSWER$,1) < > "Y" AND LEN
     (ANSWER$) > 0 THEN GOTO 10
```

The line says, "If the first letter of the response is not a Y and at least one letter has been typed in, then the phone number needs to be changed—get a new phone number."

We can add one more feature to this phone number routine to be really nice to the user: a default area code. If the user is typing in lots of numbers, saving two strokes per number represents a savings of 20%.

One way to get a default value for the area code is to build it in as a program line. If you know that the area code most likely to be used is "213," the area code for Los Angeles, then you would add

```
5  DFT$ = "213"
```

If you weren't sure and wanted the user to enter the default, then the line would read

```
5  INPUT "DEFAULT AREA CODE: ";DFT$
```

Of course, you would add error-checking and verification lines like we did above. Whichever way you prefer to do it, you would need to add the following lines as well:

```
40  VTAB 22 : REM POSITION CURSOR FOR MESSAGE
45  PRINT "PRESS RETURN FOR ";DFT$;" AREA
    CODE" : REM SHOW "OPTION" MESSAGE
90  IF NUMBER$ = CHR$ (13) OR ( NUMBER$ => "0"
    AND NUMBER$ =< "9" ) THEN GOTO 100
95  GOTO 80
```

Tricky line, that line 90! It does two things at once. First, it checks to see if a carriage return has been entered (which is ASCII code number 13). If so, it branches to 100 and goes on with the program. If a character other than a carriage return has been entered—that is, if any key *except* the RETURN or ENTER key has been pressed—the computer checks to make sure it's a number. If it is a number, then the program branches to 100 and goes on. If it isn't a number, then what was entered is illegal (since the only acceptable inputs are a carriage return or a number) and the program goes to line 90, which branches back to line 80 for another try. The number checker is in parentheses to insure that the computer evaluates the logic statements in the proper order. See your computer's programming manual for more information on logic statements and orders of precedence. Back to the code:

```
100  VTAB 22 : HTAB 1 : REM POSITION CURSOR TO
     START OF "OPTION" MESSAGE...
105  PRINT "                                    " : REM
     ENOUGH BLANKS TO CLEAR THE MESSAGE (NO
     LONGER NEEDED) FROM THE SCREEN
110  VTAB 10 : HTAB 10 : REM PUT CURSOR IN
     "INPUT" POSITION
120  IF NUMBER$ = CHR$ (13) THEN 170
```

Line 120 checks to see if the character gotten by line 80 was a carriage return. If it was, indicating that the default area code is to be used, then the routine beginning at line 170 (listed below) is executed. If not, then...

```
130  PHNE$ = PHNE$ + NUMBER$ : REM ADD THIS
     DIGIT TO THE PHONE NUMBER
```

In this case, the digit entered is the first digit in the phone number. The line could have read

```
130  PHNE$ = NUMBER$
```

and it would work just as well.

```
140  COUNT = 1 : REM ONE DIGIT IN PHONE NUMBER
150  PRINT NUMBER$; : REM SHOW THE DIGIT
160  GOTO 210 : REM SKIP LINES 170-200

165  REM DEFAULT AREA CODE ROUTINE
170  PRINT DFT$; "-...-...."; : REM DISPLAY DEFAULT
     AREA CODE & FORM
180  HTAB 14 : REM POSITION CURSOR TO RIGHT OF
     DASH
190  PHNE$ = DFT$ : REM PHONE NUMBER HAS
     DEFAULT AREA CODE
200  COUNT = 3 : REM THERE ARE THREE DIGITS IN
     THE PHONE NUMBER
```

Now you've got a nicely humanized phone routine with clear on-screen directions. Here's the whole routine:

Listing 4.3

```
0  REM PHONE NUMBER DEMO
1  REM HAS DEFAULT AREA CODE
2  REM CHECKS FOR NON-NUMBERS
3  REM PUTS IN SLASHES AUTOMATICALLY
4  REM VERIFIES NUMBER
5 DFT$ = "213": REM DEFAULT AREA CODE
10  HOME : REM CLEAR THE SCREEN
30 COUNT = 0: REM INITIALIZE A COUNTER (TO BE USED SOON)
35 PHNE$ = "": REM INIT A STRING TO HOLD THE PHONE NUMBER
40  VTAB 22
45  PRINT "PRESS RETURN FOR ";DFT$;" AREA CODE"
50  VTAB 9: HTAB 1: REM POSITION CURSOR FOR EXAMPLE
55  PRINT "EXAMPLE: 415-555-0000": REM GIVE SAMPLE TO FOLLOW
60  HTAB 3: REM POSITION CURSOR FOR FORM
65  PRINT "PHONE: ...-...-....";: REM NOTE SEMICOLON TO PREVENT CR
70  HTAB 10: REM POSITION CURSOR FOR INPUT
80  GET NUMBER$: REM WAIT FOR A CHARACTER FROM THE KEYBOARD
90  IF NUMBER$ =  CHR$ (13) OR (NUMBER$ > "0" AND NUMBER$ =  < "9") THEN  GOTO
   100
95  GOTO 80: REM ILLEGAL CHARACTER - TRY AGAIN!
100  VTAB 22: HTAB 1
105  PRINT "                                                  "
110  VTAB 10: HTAB 10
120  IF NUMBER$ =  CHR$ (13) THEN 170
130 PHNE$ = PHNE$ + NUMBER$
140 COUNT = 1
150  PRINT NUMBER$;
160  GOTO 210
170  PRINT DFT$;"-...-....";
180  HTAB 14
190 PHNE$ = DFT$
200 COUNT = 3
210  IF COUNT = 3 THEN  HTAB 11 + COUNT
220  IF COUNT = 6 THEN  HTAB 12 + COUNT
230  GET NUMBER$
240  IF NUMBER$ < "0" OR NUMBER$ > "9" THEN 230
250 COUNT = COUNT + 1
260  PRINT NUMBER$;
270 PHNE$ = PHNE$ + NUMBER$
280  IF COUNT = 10 THEN  GOTO 300
290  GOTO 210: REM GET NEXT DIGIT
300  PRINT : PRINT : INPUT "OK? (Y/N) ";ANSWER$
310  IF  LEFT$ (ANSWER$,1) <  > "Y" AND  LEN (ANSWER$) > 0 THEN  GOTO 10
320  REM REST OF PROGRAM GOES HERE
999  END
```

GETTING HELP

Programs often require more of the user than entering a date or phone number. Sometimes the instructions a user must follow are downright complex. The more complex the instructions, the more help will the user tend to require. This is especially true when the user has only just begun to use the program and is not yet familiar with all its ins and outs. We would expect that the user would keep close at hand the extensive documentation the thoughtful programmer has provided, but it still wouldn't hurt to make things a bit easier.

Help Menu

A help menu is, briefly stated, a screenpage or two of condensed instructions about a particular phase of the program's operation. Easily called by the user, it may be either RAM- or disk-based. It is usually less detailed than the printed documentation yet contains more information than is convenient to display continuously during the regular course of the program. You'll find an example of a help menu a couple of pages ahead.

The place for an extended help menu is *not* on the primary screen—the one that comes up first. Such valuable space is usually reserved for more necessary stuff. The primary page can, however, tell the user effectively and efficiently how to get help if help is available. A message like

```
PRESS CTRL H FOR HELP
```

will do nicely, but only if you make provisions in your code for the program to branch to where the help is stored!

(By the way, sometimes we can't use CTRL H for HELP because the CTRL H character causes a BACKSPACE—it's the same function and ASCII character that most micros access via the key with the left-facing arrow on it. But if you don't care about losing BACKSPACE, then by all means, feel free to use it for HELP! It seems more natural to remember H for Help than A for Aid.)

ABOUT CONTROL CHARACTERS

A control (abbreviated CTRL) character is a non-printable character usually having an ASCII value of 0-31 (CTRL characters A to Z, for instance, are ASCII codes 1-26). The control characters are accessible by pressing the CTRL key and holding it down while pressing a character. Since they don't show and therefore have very little ongoing use in a program that calls for showable characters (the usual A to Z and numbers 0 to 9), they make ideal "code" keys for branching to special routines like help menus.

> Many of these control characters have functions assigned by the computer manufacturer or in adherence to the Standard ASCII Code Assignments. A CTRL G, which is ASCII code #7, will probably ring your computer's bell. In your programs you can many times override the preassigned function of a control key and make it do whatever you want it to do.
>
> Ain't programming grand?

There should be tucked away somewhere in a page or two of memory additional specific information that the user may summon should the need occur. And perhaps there should be access to further information stored away on disk.

The Word Processor— A Typical Example

Here's a section from a word-processing program. In a word processor the user must be able to do a variety of things to the text at hand. The user must be able to type it in, to change, add, or delete words, to format left and right margins—perhaps in columns—and to arrange for various printout options. Things can really get complicated, with far too many options to keep on the screen or to expect the user to remember. It's an ideal situation for a resident help display acting as a glossary. Glossary is our name for the menu which lists the purpose of the various control keys:

Listing 4.4

```
10   HOME
100   REM (ROUTINE THAT DISPLAYS CURRENT TEXT PAGE USER IS WORKING ON)
110   VTAB 23
120   PRINT "CTRL H GETS HELP"
125   PRINT "ESC TO END";
130   VTAB 1: HTAB 1
150   GET IN$: REM ACCEPT A SINGLE CHARACTER FROM THE KEYBOARD
155   IF IN$ =  CHR$ (27) THEN  END : REM ESC ENDS IT
160   IF IN$ =  CHR$ (8) THEN  GOSUB 1000: GOTO 100: REM CHR$ (8) = CTRL H
990  TTL$ = TTL$ + IN$
995   PRINT IN$;
998   GOTO 150: REM GET ANOTHER CHARACTER
1000   REM HELP DISPLAY
1010   HOME : REM CLEAR SCREEN
1020  TITLE$ = "GLOSSARY"
1030   HTAB 21 -  LEN (TITLE$) / 2: REM ROUTINE TO CENTER TITLE$
1040   PRINT TITLE$
1050   PRINT : PRINT
1060   PRINT "CTRL D = DELETE CHARACTERS.  REPEAT CTRL D TO STOP DELETING"
1065   PRINT "CTRL E = END EDIT MODE AND RETURN TO      MAIN SELECTION MENU"

1068   PRINT "CTRL H = HELP GLOSSARY.  CALLS THIS       SCREEN"
1070   PRINT "CTRL I = INSERT CHARACTERS.  REPEAT TO    STOP INSERTING"
1080   PRINT "CTRL R = REPLACE A STRING.  FORMAT IS :   CTRL R/ OLD STRING/
    NEW STRING/ RETURN"
```

Listing 4.4 continued

```
1090  PRINT "CTRL S = SEARCH FOR A STRING"
1100  PRINT "CTRL W = WIPE OUT ALL TEXT IN MEMORY"
1110  VTAB 22: REM POSITION CURSOR TO LINE 22
1130  PRINT "PRESS RETURN TO GO BACK TO PROGRAM";
1140  GET A$: REM ACCEPT A SINGLE CHARACTER FROM KEYBOARD
1150  HOME : REM CLEAR THE SCREEN
1160  RETURN
```

The rather odd spacing in some of the PRINT statements is to make the display screen conform to our Apple's 40-column output. Programmers whose displays are more generous should make the necessary adjustments.

Line 160 checks to see if the input from the previous line is a CONTROL H. If it is, then the program branches to the glossary. We've placed access to the help menu option immediately after the GET command to demonstrate its importance. The way the program is set up, the user may access HELP any time an input is called for.

Here's what the screen looks like when the program is first run, and before anything is typed in:

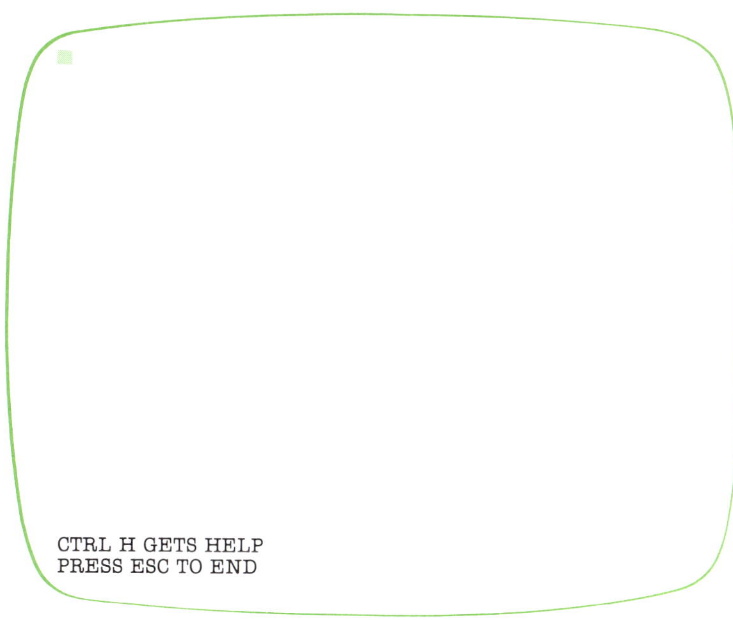

And here's what it looks like if the CTRL H is pressed (and we'll assume generous screen room here):

```
                GLOSSARY

CTRL D  = DELETE RIGHT CHARACTER
CTRL E  = END EDIT MODE AND RETURN TO
          MAIN SELECTION MENU
CTRL H  = HELP GLOSSARY. CALLS THIS
          SCREEN
CTRL I  = INSERT CHARACTERS. REPEAT TO
          STOP INSERTING
CTRL R  = REPLACE A STRING. FORMAT IS:
          CTRL R/OLD STRING/NEW
          STRING/RETURN
CTRL S  = SEARCH FOR A STRING
CTRL W  = WIPE OUT ALL TEXT IN MEMORY



PRESS SPACEBAR TO GO BACK TO PROGRAM
```

Note that the glossary, while containing adequate descriptions of the various commands, is still brief. It isn't meant to replace the hard-copy documentation but to supplement it.

Choosing Menu Mnemonics

You can also see that a menu command's symbol is the first letter of the command itself. That's no accident. The human nervous system likes order and relationship. We are more likely to remember such correspondences better than we might recall arbitrary code assignments.

We have seen programs that asked us to enter D to mean RETURN TO MAIN MENU and J for TURN ON PRINTER. Bizarre!

> Some programmers apparently assign codes in alphabetical order according to height. We recommend that you assign codes more in line with the humanity of your intended users. A little empathy goes a long way.

You can effectively use a help option whenever there are too many options to display conveniently (i.e., aesthetically), when the user might have trouble remembering all the options available, or when the options displayed are so complex that they require further explanation.

And don't forget to use short sentences.

EXPANDING HELP CONCEPTS TO DISK

Sometimes users lose track of where they put their hard-copy documentation. For those situations, having the documentation also stored on disk would be invaluable. The disk-based information could be callable as a subset of your RAM-resident help displays.

Using the word-processing example, you could add a new line:

```
1100  PRINT "ENTER '?' FOR MORE DETAILS OR"
```

You'd also need a line to check if the question mark were entered and tell what to do with it:

```
1120  IF A$ = "?" THEN GOSUB 5000 : REM
      DISKREAD SUBROUTINE
```

Now you have some choices about what to do when the program goes to line 5000. These will depend at least in part on how detailed you want the "help in more detail" to be. The simplest thing to do would be just to go out to the disk and access a file containing detailed information on all the commands listed on the RAM-resident help display—what happens to deleted characters, how the screen wraparound works in the insert mode, and so on. A more complex system of help menus is also possible. The "?" command could lead to a new question that would read

```
WHICH COMMAND DO YOU NEED MORE HELP ON?
CTRL ...
```

The user would type in a D or I or whatever command needed further explanation, and the program would retrieve from disk a few paragraphs just on that command. A combination of the two is possible, where a user could decide how much help was needed. How detailed you get is up to you and the demands of your program—the more complex the program, the more detailed will your explanations need to be. The important thing to consider is clarity for the user.

Disk Storage and Retrieval

Here are two programs designed to aid you in sending and retrieving the documentation data to and from your mass storage device (you didn't think we'd abandon you in your hour of need, did you?). The general format will work whether you're using simple or complex menu levels.

First, here's a little program for you to use to write a help file to disk. Your users won't use this program, of course. They don't want to write the directions—just to read them!

The example we use runs on the Apple II. For this system the disk commands are all preceded by D$; they will be different for all other computer systems. The algorithm (computerese for "method that we used to solve the problem") is valid for all systems. We've designed it to set up text files that work in conjunction with the Anti-splitword routine from Chapter 1.

Listing 4.5

```
0   REM STUFF-IT
1   REM PROGRAM TO STORE DOCUMENTATION TO DISK
2   REM RECALLED THROUGH "DUMP-IT"
3   REM TYPE THE WORD "END" TO MEAN "NO MORE STRINGS TO BE ENTERED"
4   REM TYPE "P" TO SET UP NEW PARAGRAPH
5 IN$ = "X": GOSUB 60000: REM ROUTINE TO ACCEPT ALL CHARACTERS
10   HOME
20   DIM A$(100): REM SET UP AN ARRAY TO HOLD 100 STRINGS OF DOCUMENTATION
30 Z = 0: REM COUNTS NUMBER OF STRINGS WRITTEN
40   CALL 768:IN$ =  MID$ (IN$,1):A$ = IN$: REM GET DOCUMENTATION STRING
50   IF A$ = "END" THEN 90: REM IF THIS IS THE LAST STRING THEN EXIT
60 Z = Z + 1: REM INCREMENT STRING COUNTER
70 A$(Z) = A$: REM SET ELEMENT Z OR ARRAY A$(*) EQUAL TO THE STRING JUST
      INPUT
80   GOTO 40: REM GET ANOTHER STRING
85   REM REST OF PROGRAM STORES STRINGS TO APPLE DISK.
90 D$ =  CHR$ (4)
95   INPUT "WHAT'S THE NAME OF THIS FILE? ";FILE$
100   PRINT D$"OPEN "FILE$
110   PRINT D$"WRITE "FILE$
120   PRINT Z
130   FOR X = 1 TO Z
140   PRINT A$(X)
150   NEXT
160   PRINT D$"CLOSE"
170   END
60000  REM ROUTINE TO ACCEPT COMMAS, COLONS, QUOTES
60001  FOR J = 768 TO 790: READ I: POKE J,I: NEXT J: DATA 162,0,32,117,253
      ,160,2,138,145,105,200,169,0,145,105,200,169,2,145,105,76,57,213
60002  RETURN
```

And here's the program to get the information back from the disk. To economize on random-access memory requirements, the program reads the data from the disk one line at a time, using only the data memory space of one string. The program prints the line on the display screen, then goes back to the disk for another line. It uses the Anti-splitword routine to make the screen formatting pleasant; the details on how that routine operates can be found in the first chapter in the section called "Broken Words." Also included is the Screenpause routine from Chapter 1, and a function at line 58360 to allow the user to stop the information flow if he or she has read enough. Again, the disk commands will have to be modified if you aren't running the program on an Apple II; see your disk manual.

Listing 4.6

```
58000  REM  DUMP-IT
58005  PRINT
58040 LIMIT = 15: REM  NUMBER OF LINES/SCREEN TO BE DISPLAYED BEFORE GOING
      TO SCREENPAUSE ROUTINE
58050 TC = 39: REM NUMBER OF COLUMNS TO BASE ANTISPLITWORD ROUTINE UPON
58060  HOME
58065 I$ = FILE$: HTAB 21 -  LEN (I$) / 2: INVERSE : PRINT I$: NORMAL : PRINT

58070 D$ =  CHR$ (4)
58080  PRINT D$"OPEN"FILE$
58090  PRINT D$"READ"FILE$
58100  INPUT Z: REM HOW MANY STRINGS?
58110  FOR X = 1 TO Z: REM DO LINES XX - YY FOR Z NUMBER OF TIMES
58120  CALL 768:IN$ =  MID$ (IN$,1):A$ = IN$
58122  REM NEXT LINE LOOKS FOR PARAGRAPH FLAG
58125  IF A$ = "P" THEN  PRINT TE$:TE$ = "": PRINT : GOTO 58280
58130  IF  LEFT$ (A$,1) <  > " " THEN A$ = " " + A$
58140 A$ = TE$ + A$
58150 Y = 0
58160 TE$ =  LEFT$ (A$,TC - Y)
58170  IF  LEN (TE$) =  LEN (A$) THEN 58280
58180  IF  RIGHT$ (TE$,1) = " " THEN  GOTO 58210
58190 Y = Y + 1
58200  GOTO 58160
58210  PRINT  LEFT$ (TE$,TC - 1)
58220 COUNT = COUNT + 1
58230  IF COUNT = LIMIT THEN  PRINT D$: GOSUB 58320: IF B$ =  CHR$ (27) THEN
      RETURN
58240 T =  LEN (A$) -  LEN (TE$)
58250  IF T = 0 THEN 58280
58260  IF A$ <  >  CHR$ (13) THEN A$ =  RIGHT$ (A$,T)
58270  GOTO 58150
58280  NEXT X
58290  PRINT TE$
58300  PRINT D$"CLOSE"FILE$
58305  VTAB 22: HTAB 1: CALL  - 958: PRINT "PRESS ANY KEY TO START...";: GET
     QUIZ$
58310  RETURN
58320  REM  SCREENPAUSE
58330  PRINT D$
58340 COUNT = 0
58350  VTAB 23
58360  PRINT "PRESS ESC TO END OR RETURN TO CONTINUE ";
58370  GET B$
58380  IF B$ =  CHR$ (27) THEN  RETURN
58390  VTAB 2: CALL  - 958: PRINT
58400  PRINT D$"READ"FILE$
58430  RETURN
```

SUMMING UP

GIVE CLEAR INSTRUCTIONS A HIGH PRIORITY

Good code, even in the most complex of programs, need not take up so much space that clarity of instruction is sacrificed. When it comes down to the crunch, do what you must to save bytes: use fewer variables, use integers rather than reals, or whatever else your computer manual says you can do. But *don't* skimp on good user directions!

REMEMBER THAT WHICH HAS BEEN WRITTEN AND PASSED FROM GENERATION TO GENERATION OF HACKERS: "FOR WHAT SHALL IT PROFITETH A PROGRAMMER WHO WINS A FEW BYTES BUT SUFFERS THE CONFUSION OF THE USER?"

or

PITHINESS IS NEXT TO GODLINESS.

MANUAL FOR YOUR NEW COMPUTER®
LEFT SIDE
SCREEN
RIGHT SIDE
PLUG
ON-OFF SWITCH
INSTRUCTIONS:
1. PLUG IN COMPUTER (SEE PLUG)
2. PROGRAM DATA
3. USE COMPUTER
ADDITIONAL INSTRUCTIONS:
4. BREATHE DEEPLY WHEN FRUSTRATED

CHAPTER 5:

HARD-COPY DOCUMENTATION

Documentation that describes software (which is unique and different from documentation that describes equipment—see the *Apple II Reference Manual* for a good example) is the aggregate of all information about the program. You've already seen information about on-screen directions and help menus (including help stored in disk text files) elsewhere in this book. This chapter concerns itself exclusively with the printed hard-copy documentation you would supply with your program.

Please realize that we would have to write an entire book to do justice to the subject of hard-copy documentation. Our intention here is to make you aware of the subject, to see that you become familiar with the bare bones of documentation, and to encourage you to write documentation that is thorough and geared to your program's intended users. Thus we cover the *minimum* requirements of printed documentation for applications programs.

Keeping that in mind, you should realize that all documentation worth its ink should tell all of the following about the program:

1. How to find your way around the documentation itself
2. What the program does
3. What equipment you need to get it working
4. How to get it working and how to make it stop
5. How to get more help
6. Special information about non-standard features
7. Copyright status

We'll cover each of these subjects in turn, and so that you can take steps to ensure that you reap the benefits of your work, we have included information about securing copyrights for your program and documentation.

THE PROBLEM

Good documentation allows a user to determine whether the program is likely to fill the user's need and, if it does, how best to use the program. Unfortunately, most software comes with very little documentation, and too often even that is muddy and inadequate. The frustration a user feels in those situations is hard to describe. It's like giving an instructionless chess set to a couple of Martians and telling them to have fun!

It's impossible to overemphasize the importance of thorough documentation. Without it your users are unlikely to get the full benefit of your coding, although they are likely to want to throttle you for setting them up for frustration.

To be sure, different programs have different requirements. A database management package will, in general, demand much more thorough documentation than will a piece of software that computes simple interest on a savings account. The more complex the program and varied the user options, the more detailed need be the instructions you provide. It's nearly impossible to provide too much documentation. The user can always skip material that's not necessary to the immediate purpose—but if what's needed *isn't* there or is really hard to find?

DOCUMENTATION AIDS

It would seem a shame if, after you'd worked long and hard on your documentation, your user couldn't find a particular piece of necessary information because there were no "maps to facts" to follow. That's where documentation aids come in. We'll talk briefly about four aids: table of contents, index, reference card, and glossary.

Table of Contents

This will appear at the head of your documentation. It is the same as a table of contents in a book. Essentially it is a listing of major topics (sometimes with a brief description) followed by the page number where each topic appears. The topics are listed in sequential (as opposed to alphabetical) order. Sometimes the major topics are followed by subtopics with their own page references, but this is seldom required unless your documentation is very extensive or quite detailed. (The extent and detail of the documentation is, of course, a function of the complexity of your program. The more complex the program, the more detailed the documentation needs to be.) The purpose of the table of contents is to act as a quick reference to broad information areas:

Table of Contents

SUBJECT	PAGE
INTRODUCTION	1
SYSTEM REQUIREMENTS	2
LOADING THE PROGRAM	2
SETTING UP CATEGORIES	3
ENTERING DATA	6
CHANGING FILES	10

Index

An index, on the other hand, is a detailed reference list appearing at the end of the documentation. It consists of a list of the most important terms used, with each term followed by the numbers of all pages on which it appears. It is more extensive than the table of contents and appears in alphabetical order. It is amazingly useful if it is complete:

Index

androids, 6, 8, 14
articles, 2, 7, 9, 13, 14
.
.
.
data, 1, 5, 7, 8
directory, 17
.
.
.
printer, 1, 11
.
.
reading disk, 3, 9, 14

Thus if our users need to find out what kind of a printer works with this program, they need only check pages 1 and 11—the only places where printers are mentioned. Most non-fiction books contain indexes. Check one to see in more detail what we're talking about.

Reference Card

This is simply a shorthand compilation of the major program features and options. It acts as a memory jogger and a quick reference for the user. Using a text editor example:

EDITING FUNCTIONS

CTRL A—Add a line	p. 5
CTRL B—Block move (requires markers)	p. 5
CTRL D—Delete character	p. 6
CTRL I—Insert characters (see CTRL T)	p. 8
.	
.	
.	
CTRL T—Terminate character insert (see CTRL I)	p. 12

The first column holds the command word, the second column the command definition, and the third column the documentation page reference for detailed explanation. A similar form could be constructed for entry parameters in data bases (number of characters per field, character types allowed, etc.) and for special disk-access codes.

The number of charts needed, and indeed whether any charts are needed at all, depends on the program's complexity and the number of commands available to the user. The greater the variety of commands, the greater the need for effective mnemonics.

We assume that the user has read and studied your extensive documentation (although that's one heck of an assumption) so that the charts are merely reminders. Some good data-base programs, text editors, and language systems have tear-off reference cards at the back of their manuals. See these for more examples of what summary charts should look like.

Glossary

The final aid is the glossary. It is an alphabetical dictionary of terms used in the documentation. It usually contains no page references. A glossary is especially important in situations where the intended user is new to computers and you use some technical terms that might not be understood. A glossary is also necessary if you use terms not generally known to computer users.

Not all documentation requires all four types of aids. Just remember the basic rule:

> MORE DOCUMENTATION IS ALMOST ALWAYS BETTER THAN LESS.

THE PROGRAM'S PURPOSE AND DEFINITION

The next thing documentation should cover is what the program is supposed to do. Here's the opening statements of a typical example:

> MEDIMASTER is a data-base management system designed specifically for medical professionals interested in the cataloging of medical publications...

Note that this first paragraph doesn't go into too much detail. Its purpose is to let the potential user know what the program is about. It begins with the program's name, followed by the program's general category (data-base management system), its intended user (medicos), and its specific use (catalog for medical articles).

The next paragraph should briefly describe program features—in this case how many areas, how many subheads in each area, and so on. These describe the limitations of the program, which are important to state early on. While the first paragraph says *what* the program does, this second paragraph tells *how much* it can do. A user will usually determine whether this program fits the need based on these first two paragraphs:

> ...It provides facilities for storing synopses of up to 5000 articles in 15 major medical areas. Areas covered include three sections on diagnosis, three on treatment modalities, four on pharmacology, four on office management and one on real estate. Provisions are included for 15 subsections under each major area and options for five more...

Note that we describe the parameters *briefly* here. We don't say what areas fall under "diagnosis" or how many characters are allowed in each subheading. We certainly will cover these things later, but they are not needed here.

WHAT EQUIPMENT THE PROGRAM REQUIRES

The next paragraph should describe the system the software runs on. Some computer professionals we've talked with prefer to see this information displayed even earlier, perhaps on the first page of the documentation. We can't argue with them. No matter how early you show it, this section should be complete:

> MEDIMASTER requires an Apple Z with a FORTHSOFT card, 512k-word RAM and at least one 5-inch micro-Winchester hard disk system with streaming cassette tape backup/loader. A letter-quality medium speed (300 lines/minute) printer is recommended, but any printer capable of printing 80 columns is acceptable. As set up here, the program runs under ZOS 8.7

Our example includes the make and model of computer (Apple Z), language (FORTH) and any special subset or parameter (read-only-memory [ROM] resident), random-access memory (RAM) requirements (512k), mass storage device requirements (five-inch hard disk and backup tape), and any special peripherals (80-column printer). The particular version of a disk operating system is also given. *All of this information is absolutely necessary.* There are many computers on the market in many configurations speaking many subsets and supersets of many languages, and the chances are your program won't match them all.

Remember to say everything that your system requires. If your program is set up for telecommunications and includes special control codes, then you need to specify in this section the purpose of these codes.

OPERATING INSTRUCTIONS

In most cases, this section of your documentation should be the longest. It tells the user how to make the program do at least what you as the creator can make the program do.

That's not as hard as it might seem. Nobody expects you to be Socrates when all you have to be is complete, clear, and logical (that is, organized) in your approach.

Determine Your Audience

The first task is to discover for whom you are writing. Zero in on your user. Are the users computer-sophisticated or computer-naive or in between? Are they adults or children? What can you assume about the users' educational levels?

The character of your audience will determine how detailed your explanations must be. If the user is sophisticated, you need not describe what the ENTER key is about, or where it is on the keyboard. Nor do you need to warn about touching the exposed read-write slot on a floppy disk. If, however, your intended user is a first-time or only lightly experienced computer user, then you must describe almost everything in detail. If the user is a child, it is inappropriate to use words like "inappropriate" in your descriptions because it is unlikely a child would know what the word means. Writing instructions for an eight-year-old child should be far different from writing for a Ph.D. in Computer Science (most of the time, anyway).

Of course, much of this might already be determined by the nature of your program. A metacompiler generator obviously calls for different documentation than does a program that reviews adding and subtracting single-digit numbers.

> THE TONE AND DICTION OF YOUR EXPLANATIONS MUST MATCH THE ABILITY OF YOUR USER TO RELATE TO THEM. OTHERWISE YOU MIGHT JUST AS WELL WRITE IN SANSKRIT.

Begin at the Beginning and When You Reach the End, Stop

Having determined your audience, the next step is to begin your explanation. A good place to begin is with what the user sees first as the program is run. Then proceed through the program in sequential order from the user's standpoint of interaction. "Sequential order" means what steps the typical first-time user would take to use the program most effectively.

Let's assume that your program is a text editor that allows a user to enter data, change it, store it to disk, and print it. It would *not* be effective to begin by explaining how to print a file. The first directions would more appropriately deal with getting started—how to start the program, get into "enter" mode, and enter data. Next would come sections on how to change what's been entered, how to store and retrieve from disk, and finally how to get a printout. You explain the program in the order the user would go through it.

If each major section has subsections, explain them in the same way. Continuing with our text-editor example, the CHANGE section might have commands to change, add, move, and delete single characters, whole lines, and whole paragraphs. Go from smallest to largest, particular to general. Or go from largest to smallest, general to particular! "Whatever is appropriate" is the way to go. The important thing here is order and consistency.

> THE HUMAN NERVOUS SYSTEM HAS A FONDNESS FOR THAT WHICH IS ORDERLY AND LOGICAL, SO YOU MIGHT AS WELL GO WITH YOUR USER'S BUILT-IN EQUIPMENT.

Follow this pattern from the first time the user touches the computer right to the very end of the program, when you'll explain how the user exits the software. Leave no option unexamined, no element of screen display unexplained, no command undetailed. Don't leave out a thing! Talk about the ON switch, inserting the disk into the drive, and the boot process. If it has to do with the operation of the program and if it's appropriate to your audience, talk about it!

Give a Guided Tour and Make the User Drive the Bus

There are several approaches you could use to present the program instructions. You could use an outline, straight exposition, etc. Whatever you're most comfortable with will probably work to some degree, providing you follow the recommendations we just gave you. But we have found the method that provides the quickest learning with the least amount of hassle is the *interactive tutorial*. You literally walk your user through the program step-by-step, giving actual hands-on experience as you go. In fact, we even call this type of tutorial a "walkthrough." The user gets to try every function as it is being explained, ensuring that what has just been read is immediately reinforced. And that means the user gets the full benefit of your program right from the beginning.

Here's how to do it, continuing with the text-editor example:

> Here we are in the DATA ENTRY mode. Type in a few lines just to get the feel of things. Make your last line "computers make great toys."
>
> We'll use the DELETE function (CTRL D) to take out the word "toys." Using the ESC sequence spoken of earlier, place the cursor over the "t" (use the cursor control keys as we learned earlier). Now press CTRL D four times and—*voilá*— "toys" is gone! Note that the text has been closed up and all the letters after where "toys" was have been moved backwards (look, Ma—no holes).
>
> WARNING—IF YOU ARE AT THE END OF YOUR FILE AND YOU CONTINUE TO USE THE DELETE FUNCTION, UNPREDICTABLE RESULTS WILL OCCUR.
>
> Let's move on to INSERT (CTRL I)...

As you can see, each function is handled individually, with the user not just reading about doing something, but actually doing it. If while reading the first four chapters of this book you tried the various examples at your computer, you've already experienced the effectiveness of an interactive tutorial (we hope).

Note that we talk about what should be happening on the screen (the spaces "closing up" over the no-longer-existing word) to make sure the user is with us. Also note that in the above example we included an appropriate warning message. Such cautions should be included wherever they apply.

Follow this tutorial style of explanation for every section of your program. Be sure to give at least one example or experience for *every* feature in the program. Even if a feature seems absurdly obvious to you, there's a user out there somewhere who will manage to misunderstand it unless you lead a tour through it at least once.

This walkthrough method may be tedious to write, but it will pay off in terms of ease for the user and goodwill for you. Take our word for it—your efforts will be appreciated!

FEATURES REVISITED—DEFAULTS, RULE-VIOLATIONS, AND OTHER CRIMES

Although you may (should) have included this information as it became appropriate in the body of your operating instructions, it's a good idea to restate in a summarized form what will happen if the program "rules" are violated. Include here all parameters, defaults, and consequences of rule infractions. What happens if the computer is looking for an entry and the user presses the RETURN or ENTER key without typing any other character? What if the input has a limit of 10 characters and the user enters 12? What will happen if the user enters an alphabetic (A–Z) in a numeric (0–9) field? The chapters on error trapping in this manual cover these issues in some detail, but that information must also be included in the hard copy. For example:

> ...a default condition occurs when the user presses the RETURN key without entering any other data in response to a query from the computer. Default on 'YES/NO' questions is 'YES' unless otherwise stated on screen. There are no other defaults, so the program will ignore an empty RETURN and wait for valid data to be entered...
>
> ...NAMES must be between five and 28 characters long. If fewer than five characters are entered the program will ignore the too-short NAME and again ask for a valid NAME entry longer than five characters. All characters beyond the 28th will be ignored by the computer. If more than 28 characters are entered the computer will assume the first 28 are valid and will store the NAME accordingly...

Fatal Error Warnings

It is *most* important that a user know what will crash the program. Of course, if you have written your program in accordance with the rules and examples laid down elsewhere in this book, you will already have eliminated most of the potential trouble spots. But if there is some error you can't protect against, then tell the user about it. For example:

> ...pressing the RESET key while the disk drive is in operation will cause the file to be erased and the program will stop. Restarting will be necessary...
>
> ...Using the file called BEESWAX as an EXEC will destroy the major INDEX...
>
> ...restating a name in the CHANGE section without updating the RECORDS file will throw the pointers off and the program will abort...

Note that the above are examples of what we are calling *non-trappable* errors, errors that fall outside our ability as programmers to prevent. The ideas is for us to catch as many potential trouble spots as we can and warn the user about the rest.

Crash Recovery

You can extend a real service to the user by revealing what to do to save any new data if the program crashes in the middle of a session:

> ...if you hit the RESET key during a WRITE cycle, you might still save your data. From the monitor type "800G." Then type "GOTO 1250." Line 1250 writes the data in memory to disk...
>
> ...an OUT Of DATA error during a DISK READ cycle might indicate that you have replaced the data in a particular record with an ASCII null character. You might be able to retrieve the other records in the file by 'jumping' over the empty record. To do that follow this procedure...

It shouldn't be too hard for you to provide this recovery data. If you're like us, you know about these fatal errors (and what to do about them) from your own experience!

GETTING MORE HELP

Chances are you won't be able to come up with every way a user can crash your program, so you won't be able to provide all the rescues. It's a good idea, therefore, to include some way for a user to get help in case of desperate straits. The easiest way for users to get help is through the company that distributes your program. Your documentation should therefore include the distributor's address and, if possible, a phone number. The company can run "interference" for you by dealing with people who have misread the documentation or who have other problems not directly related to your program. When your distributor does find out about real bugs, you can be contacted by the company. When you solve the programming problem, you send your distributor the corrected code; the distributor then takes whatever steps are neccessary to correct the copies of your program already in the hands of users.

If you are distributing the program yourself, then include a post office box where users can write to you. It might be unwise to include your home phone number, however, since some people forget that programmers sleep.

Even if you don't expect any fatal errors, it's still a good idea to include a contact address. Somebody might discover a varmint in your program.

Forget not Lubarsky's Law of Cybernetic Entomology:

"THERE'S ALWAYS ONE MORE BUG"

[from Arthur Block, *Murphy's Law* (Los Angeles: Price/Stern/Sloan, 1979), p.39]

SPECIAL DESCRIPTIONS AND INSTRUCTIONS

Use this section to describe any special information not covered elsewhere. Going back to the Medimaster example where we talked about special control codes, this would be the place to explain (step-by-step, of course) how to change the code for special applications. If your program requires a printer and has within it code for operating a serial unit, you might want to explain how to hook up a parallel one.

If your software is actually a system comprised of a number of programs, you would here explain the function of each program. If the software creates special utility files as it goes along, they too would be described here.

If you have a number of such special situations, use a separate section with a separate heading for each one. That makes it easier for the user to find the needed information.

COPYRIGHT INFORMATION

Finally, you should provide data on the copyright status of your program and documentation.

Copyrighting a program is a way of protecting yourself from being ripped off. When you copyright your program, you are declaring it a piece of original work. You are saying that you hold the rights to copying the program, selling and distributing it, or just giving it away if that's what you choose to do. Holding a copyright allows you to sue people who violate your copyright. If you win the case (and holding the copyright gives your case a lot of strength), the court will probably order the violators to repay you what funds you lost because of their actions. In some cases, the court may award you damages as well. What that actually means in terms of dollars and cents is up to the court. Securing a copyright is simple. First, you contact your local Federal Information Office and ask them to send you federal copyright form TX. If you don't have a local FIO, you can write to:

United States Copyright Office
Library of Congress
Washington, D.C. 20559

Fill out the form and send it along with one listing of your program, two copies of the documentation, and the copyright fee (currently $10.00) to the copyright office.

Your copyright is good until 50 years after you have left this mortal coil and is valid throughout all of Europe, the British Commonwealth of Nations, Russia, most Communist countries, and Japan. Much of South America is not covered.

If your material is copyrighted, you should include a notice like this one:

> PROGRAM AND DOCUMENTATION COPYRIGHT © 1981
> JOHN SCRIBBLEMONGER AND XYZ COMPANY
> -COMMERCIAL RIGHTS RESERVED-

The notice must include the copyright symbol © or the word copyright or the abbreviation COPR., the name of the person or company holding the copyright, and the year of first publication. So that your users can be clear on what rights they have to copy the program or give it away, it's a good idea to include a statement about what rights are being held and what rights are "given up." In the above example, only the commercial rights are reserved. This is the kind of statement you'll often see at the head of program listings published in the popular computer magazines. It means that the copyright holder has granted the public the right to copy the program out of the magazine and to use it as a personal tool (or game or whatever) but that no one except the copyright holder may sell the program or use it for any money-making purpose. If the copyholder didn't want to give up any rights at all, then the statement would read

> -ALL RIGHTS RESERVED-

If you don't mind the program and documentation getting around, then substitute

> PROGRAM AND DOCUMENTATION IN THE PUBLIC DOMAIN

for the copyright and reserved lines. This line means that anybody can do anything they want to with the program, including selling it.

CONCLUSION

In this chapter we've tried to impress upon you the need for good program documentation. We've attempted to show you what you must include, but we haven't by any means exhausted the subject.

As we said before, assuming the documentation is "well-mapped," more documentation is better than less.

Don't limit yourself to our ideas and formats—add your own! The idea is to provide clear and complete directions geared to the sophistication—or lack of it—of your intended users.

After all, they're only human.

A COMPUTER IS ONLY AS BRILLIANT AS THE HUMAN WHO PROGRAMS IT
WHERE WERE YOU WHEN I NEEDED YOU

CONCLUSION: A SUMMARY OF OUR METHODS

Here's a synopsis describing the major subjects of each chapter, what user-friendly techniques we proposed, and what methods, warnings, and people-oriented bonuses we recommended to make the techniques more interactive and humanized. All proposed methods can be found described in detail with BASIC examples in the appropriate chapter. Examples of all the techniques and methods can be found in the listings of STATES & CAPITALS and ELECTRONIC PHONE PAD in Appendices II and III respectively. You'll find a summary example of Chapter 5 in Appendix III's *EPP Operator's Manual*. Keep in mind that all the techniques might be used as solutions to a variety of problems. Don't limit yourself to the categories we establish; they're meant to spur your imagination, not limit it.

CHAPTER 1: SCREEN FORMATTING FOR CLARITY

The main emphasis in this chapter was using the various features of the computer's display to communicate effectively with the operator. We recommended that you be orderly and clear in your displays and that you recognize that there's a strong relationship between aesthetic presentation and human understanding.

PROBLEM: how to tell what program's about
SOLUTION: provide a title page
METHOD: centering, blocking, left and right justifying, highlighting

PROBLEM: how to make clear what on-screen information is most important
SOLUTION: make important text stand out from background
METHOD: centering, highlighting, bordering
WARNING: use high attention-getters like FLASH and BEL sparingly, lest they become ineffective and offensive

PROBLEM: how to present information in aesthetically pleasing ways
SOLUTION: present text as it might appear in a book
METHOD: line up numerics around decimals, avoid broken words, provide paging

CHAPTER 2: CRASHPROOFING

This chapter's theme was trapping bad inputs that might be fatal to the program. We suggested that the best way to handle potential problems was to set up a buffer zone between the input and processing stages of your program. We said that there were three general steps you needed to take: 1) use only STRING inputs, 2) compare INPUT data to pre-established limits, and 3) in case an error was detected, give friendly error messages and prompt for new inputs.

PROBLEM: RETURN is the only key pressed in response to input request
SOLUTION: provide DEFAULT values or reject "empty" inputs
METHOD: use STRING inputs only and compare to allowable preset parameters

PROBLEM: too many or too few characters entered
SOLUTION: count the characters entered before processing
METHOD: use LEN function and compare to allowable preset parameters
BONUS: show how many characters are allowed ("NAME: . .")

PROBLEM: alphabetic entered where number was requested
SOLUTION: make sure it's a number before processing
METHOD: use STRING input and compare to ASCII code range 48-57 (see Appendix I for ASCII chart)

PROBLEM: space bar accidently hit before or after entering string of letters
SOLUTION: filter out leading and trailing spaces before processing
METHOD: Use LEN and check for CHR$(32) or " " (they're the same)

PROBLEM: operator types in misspelled or wrong word from word-based menu
SOLUTION: use only numeric menus
METHOD: number each menu choice and compare input to allowable preset parameters

CHAPTER 3: VERIFICATIONS AND VALIDATIONS

Our main emphasis here was trapping incorrect inputs that might invalidate a user's data. Our primary suggestion was that you allow the operator to change inputs before processing input data and that you permit changes in data at a later time as well.

PROBLEM: operator discovers error right after input
SOLUTION: catch input before processing, get OK before going on
METHOD: Use GET for single-character confirmation ("N" response gets input again)
BONUS: keep old input information displayed and allow RETURN only to accept old data

PROBLEM: operator discovers input number X in series of inputs is wrong
SOLUTION: allow operator to back up and reenter "bad" data
METHOD: reconfirm entire series of input data before final storage or processing
BONUS: display old information, allow RETURN only to accept old data, provide CLEAR LINE option

PROBLEM: operator discovers input is wrong only after all data has been processed and stored
SOLUTION: allow for correction as in foregoing procedure
METHOD: same as above
BONUS: same as above
WARNING: check if all data must be reprocessed to account for corrected input

CHAPTER 4: DIRECTIONS ON THE DISPLAY

Helping the operator understand how to use the program was this chapter's subject matter. Simply put, we suggested you provide on-screen directions in words and symbols that were clear and simple. We showed you how to do that using both random-access and disk memory.

PROBLEM: operator is faced with menu of choices and doesn't know how to proceed
SOLUTION: provide brief screen message like "ENTER NUMBER NEXT TO YOUR CHOICE"
METHOD: display highlighted or other prominent way
WARNING: make mnemonics logical (? for HELP, P for PRINTER, etc.)

PROBLEM: operator still doesn't know what to do
SOLUTION: provide option for further help
METHOD: special character causes more information to be displayed
BONUS: allows third level of help to be read in from disk if program warrants
WARNING: let operator know more help is available ("ENTER A QUESTION MARK FOR MORE HELP")

PROBLEM: input format is confusing or ambiguous
SOLUTION: provide precise example of expected format
METHOD: display a form to fill out (''DATE:—/—/—'')
BONUS: computer automatically types in slashes and spaces while inputs likely to repeat have default values (e.g., dates, area codes)

PROBLEM: operator can't figure out how to exit current routine or program
SOLUTION: keep EXIT options on screen
METHOD: one or two keystrokes should end (use seldom-used character like ESC or ^)

CHAPTER 5: HARD-COPY DOCUMENTATION

The final chapter concerned itself with providing sufficient printed matter to allow the operator to get the most out of your program. We exhorted you to make sure every aspect of the program that might be important to the operator was described in detail, and we tried to emphasize that more documentation is almost always better than less. When in doubt, describe it in detail.

PROBLEM: program needs specialized equipment to operate
SOLUTION: describe program requirements in extreme detail
METHOD: set up PROGRAM REQUIREMENTS section close to beginning of documentation

PROBLEM: documentation is extensive and specific information is hard to locate
SOLUTION: provide reference aids
METHOD: develop table of contents, command summary card, index

PROBLEM: documentation uses many specialized terms
SOLUTION: simplify terms and provide definitions
METHOD: develop glossary

PROBLEM: program is complex and hard for beginner to use
SOLUTION: show step-by-step how to use
METHOD: include a tutorial
BONUS: make tutorial a ''walkthrough'' with consistent examples used

PROBLEM: program might be used with a variety of equipment
SOLUTION: make sure all options are covered with interfacing techniques described
METHOD: set up special section

THE BOTTOM LINE: OUR HIDDEN CURRICULUM

Educators often refer to the "hidden curriculum" when they talk about course development. The hidden curriculum is what is taught beyond the subject matter, what is implied, although perhaps never stated directly. In *APPLE BACKPACK: Humanized Programming in BASIC*, we've tried to teach you how to write programs that anybody can use. We also had a hidden curriculum. We tried to bridge the gap between machines and people.

We hope we've shown that the proper use of high technology is service to humanity, that high technology and everyday people can and should get along together, and that everybody ought to be able to take advantage of our greatest scientific accomplishments. We'll be satisfied that we've succeeded in teaching our hidden curriculum when we begin to see programs that, by their very form, say

```
THIS PROGRAM FOR HUMANS—NO EXPERIENCE
NECESSARY.
```

APPENDIX I: ASCII CHART

Decimal	Character
000	NUL
001	SCH
002	STX
003	ETX
004	EOT
005	ENQ
006	ACK
007	BEL
008	BS
009	HT
010	LF
011	VT
012	FF
013	CR
014	SO
015	SI
016	DLE
017	DC1
018	DC2
019	DC3
020	DC4
021	NAK
022	SYN
023	ETB
024	CAN
025	EM
026	CONTROL
027	ESCAPE
028	FS
029	GS
030	RS
031	US
032	SPACE
033	!
034	"
035	#

Decimal	Character
036	$
037	%
038	&
039	'
040	(
041	)
042	*
043	+
044	'(right apostrophe)
045	-
046	.
047	/
048	0
049	1
050	2
051	3
052	4
053	5
054	6
055	7
056	8
057	9
058	:
059	;
060	<
061	=
062	>
063	?
064	@
065	A
066	B
067	C
068	D
069	E

Decimal	Character
070	F
071	G
072	H
073	I
074	J
075	K
076	L
077	M
078	N
079	O
080	P
081	Q
082	R
083	S
084	T
085	U
086	V
087	W
088	X
089	Y
090	Z
091	[
092	\
093	]
094	^ (or ↑)
095	(underscore)
096	‘ (left apostrophe)
097	a
098	b
099	c
100	d
101	e
102	f
103	g

Decimal	Character	Decimal	Character	Decimal	Character
104	h	112	p	120	x
105	i	113	q	121	y
106	j	114	r	122	z
107	k	115	s	123	{
108	l	116	t	124	|
109	m	117	u	125	}
110	n	118	v	126	~
111	o	119	w	127	DEL

LF=Line Feed FF=Form Feed CR=Carriage Return DEL=Rubout

CONTROL CHARACTERS					
NUL	Null	**LF**	Line Feed	**SYN**	Synchronous Idle
SOH	Start of Heading	**VT**	Vertical Tabulation	**ETB**	End of Transmission Block
STX	Start of Text	**FF**	Form Feed	**CAN**	Cancel
ETX	End of Text	**CR**	Carriage Return	**EM**	End of Medium
EOT	End of Transmission	**SO**	Shift Out	**SUB**	Substitute
ENQ	Enquiry	**SI**	Shift In	**ESC**	Escape
ACK	Acknowledge	**DLE**	Data Link Escape	**FS**	File Separator
BEL	Bell (audible or attention signal)	**DC1**	Device Control 1	**GS**	Group Separator
BS	Backspace	**DC2**	Device Control 2	**RS**	Record Separator
HT	Horizontal Tabulation (punched card skip)	**DC3**	Device Control 3	**US**	Unit Separator
		DC4	Device Control 4 (Stop)	**DEL**	Delete
		NAK	Negative Acknowledge		

IF **YOU** WIN... I'LL RUN A STATISTICAL ANALYSIS OF YOUR LATEST DATA
IF **I** WIN... YOU SHAVE OFF YOUR BEARD

APPENDIX II: STATES AND CAPITALS

STATES AND CAPITALS is a fun-to-use learning program we wrote to illustrate many concepts of humanized programming. Its emphasis is on-screen formatting and it has some interesting little special effects. It's simple to use and requires no hard-copy documentation since all the instructions for the program are kept in random-access memory (RAM).

WHAT THE PROGRAM DOES AND WHOM IT'S FOR

In its present form, STATES AND CAPITALS is a game whose subject matter and instructions are written for kids around 12 years old. There's a section later on to show you how to modify it for other subject matter and age groups. The following is a copy of the instructions to the program (retrieved by the operator by pressing the letter I at the appropriate time). We'll add some screen displays so you can see part of what you'll get after you've entered the code. It loses a lot in the translation from dynamic computer to static book, but you'll get the idea:

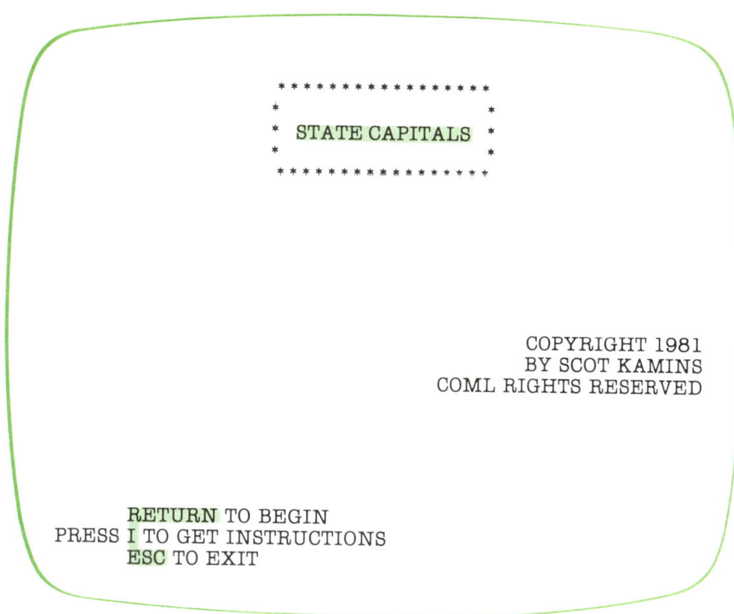

This is a game you play against the computer. The object of the game is to guess the capital of the state displayed on the computer screen. If you guess correctly on the first try, your side gets ten points.

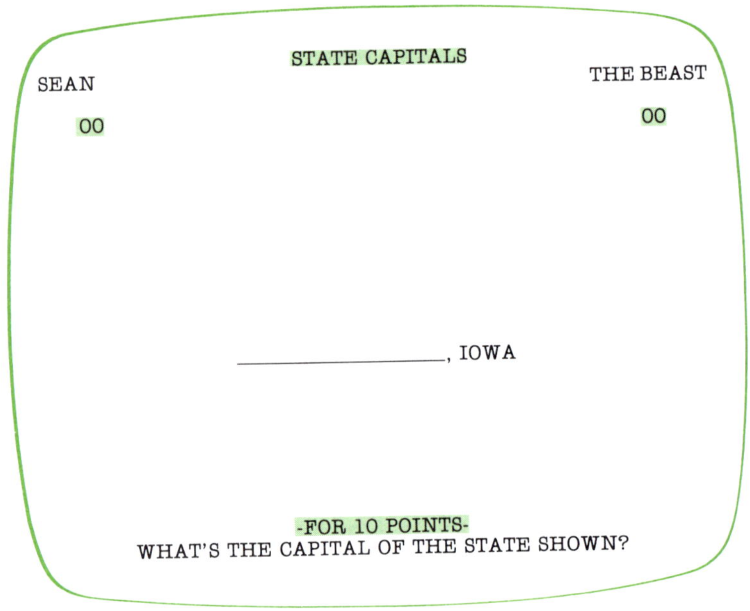

If your first guess is wrong, the computer will show you the names of three capital cities. One of them is the right one. If you choose correctly, you get five points.

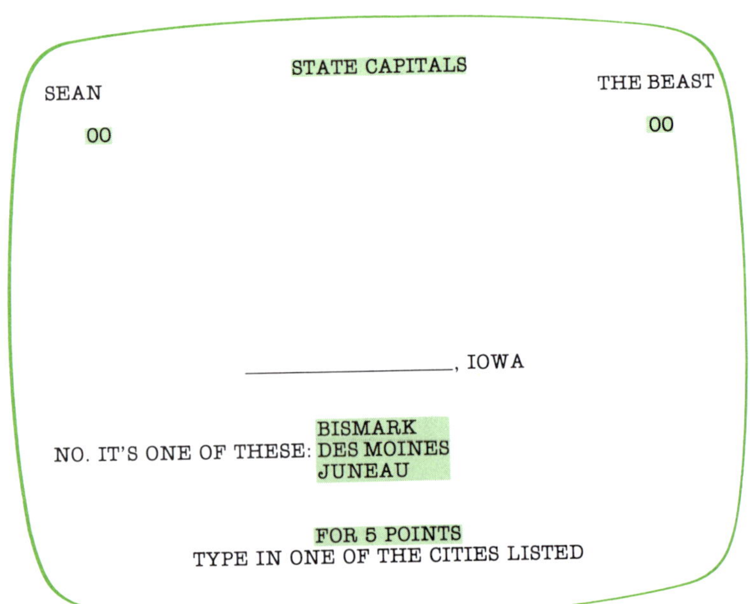

But if you guess wrong, the computer (called "THE BEAST") gets ten points!

The computer will choose 10 states at random to present to you, one each turn. After each turn, you can see a list of all the states and their capitals (if you want to).

```
                     STATE CAPITALS
SEAN                                              THE BEAST

     45                                                30
DES MOINES IA                                 BISMARK ND
OKLAHOMA CITY OK                               TOPEKA KS
LANSING MI                                   COLUMBUS OH
SPRINGFIELD IL
PHOENIX AZ


   CAPITAL                 STATE                (ABBREV)

MONTGOMERY              ALABAMA                   (AL)
JUNEAU                  ALASKA                    (AK)
PHOENIX                 ARIZONA                   (AZ)
LITTLE ROCK             ARKANSAS                  (AR)
SACRAMENTO              CALIFORNIA                (CA)
DENVER                  COLORADO                  (CO)
PRESS ANY KEY FOR MORE (ESC STOPS LIST)
```

The computer will keep score for you (and for itself) so you can see how you're doing. It will also show you which ones you got right and which ones you got wrong—the ones awarded to THE BEAST! Good luck!

```
                     STATE CAPITALS
SEAN                                              THE BEAST

     45                                                30
AUSTIN TX                                     BISMARK ND
JUNEAU AK                                      PIERRE SD
JEFFERSON CITY MO                              LINCOLN NE
TRENTON NJ                                 LITTLE ROCK AR
CARSON CITY NV
PROVIDENCE RI


SEAN WINS!



ANOTHER ROUND? (Y/N)
```

EQUIPMENT NEEDS

The program will run in any Apple II computer system with 16K of memory and Applesoft in read-only memory (ROM) or language card. No disk system is required since the program may be saved to and loaded from tape.

FOR THE PROGRAMMER

Special Apple II Stuff

Some of the code used in this program refers to routines resident in the Apple II's monitor ROM. Here is a list of those references, including the line where the code first appears, the code itself, and what the code does:

LINE	CODE	
60	PEEK (37)	Holds cursor's current vertical position
410	CALL -868	Clears screen to end of current line
560	CALL -958	Clears screen to end of page
824	POKE -16368, 0	Clears accidental keypress before "GET"
36060	PEEK (-16336)	Click speaker once

Special Subroutines and Program Lines

Here's a list of subroutines and lines used in the program making use of techniques described in *APPLE BACKPACK: Humanized Programming in BASIC*. Some techniques are used so frequently and in so many places (highlighting and on-screen directions, for instance) that it doesn't make sense to reference them all, so we just deal with the major ones here. Included are program line number, the routine's name, and a reference back to the book's chapter.

LINE	PURPOSE	CHAPTER
50	BROKEN WORDS	CH. 1
60	ASCII CODE	CH. 2
870	HIGHLIGHTING	CH. 1
29010	CHARACTER LENGTH FORM	CH. 2
29070	''ACCEPT OLD DATA'' DEFAULT	CH. 3
29150	CONFIRM DATA ENTRY	CH. 3
29250	TRUNCATE TOO-LONG STRINGS	CH. 2
30000	TITLE PAGE	CH. 1
30305	MENU MNEMONICS	CH. 4
30450	REJECT UNACCEPTABLE INPUT	CH. 2
30500	LEADING, TRAILING SPACES	CH. 2
30260	ON-SCREEN DIRECTIONS	CH. 4
31000	BORDERING	CH. 1
33000	RIGHT JUSTIFY	CH. 1
34000	CENTERING	CH. 1
35050	JUSTIFY NUMBERS	CH. 1
37000	GETTING HELP	CH. 4
50000	RAM-RESIDENT DIRECTIONS	CH. 4

Data Set Locations

You might want to change some of the ''cheers'' that appear on the screen each time either side scores points (our cheers were written for computer-sophisticated kids). Or you might decide that our directions are too simple or too complex. We keep all such information in DATA statements. Here are the names of the data sets, their line locations, and the names of the arrays into which they get loaded (and we all need to get loaded once in a while):

DATA SET	LINES	ARRAY NAMES
CAPITALS	60000-60049	CAPITAL$(*)
STATES	60000-60049	STAET$(*)
STATE ABBREVIATIONS	60000-60049	ABBREV$(*)
CHEERS FOR THE BEAST	60100-60104	BEAST$(*)
CHEERS FOR THE HUMAN	60200-60114	HUMAN$(*)
GAME INSTRUCTIONS	60200-60300	(NO ARRAY)

Notice how the data is arranged in these sets and how they correspond to the ''array loading lines'' (210 and 215). Be sure to keep these correspondences when you change the data sets.

Making a "Universal Match Game"

STATES AND CAPITALS is easy to change into a more flexible teaching tool. In fact, in less than 10 minutes (excluding the time it takes to type in new data sets) you can change the code so that any "matching pairs" can be taught. Call your new game "EUROPEAN CAPITALS" or "BOOKS AND AUTHORS" or "HEROS AND PLAYS"—whatever is appropriate for your matching pairs.

First, here are the locations of specialized words used in PRINT statements you'll have to change to match your new game:

CITIES: 710
STATES: 460, 823, 980, 30470, 37020
CAPITALS: 460, 823, 37020
STATE CAPITALS: 260, 30010, 30420
ABBREVIATION: 37020

Second, you may want to modify the lines where we display all states, capitals, and state name abbreviations:

ALL DATA DISPLAY HEADING: 37020
ALL DATA DISPLAY PRINTOUT: 37060
ALL DATA ARRAY LOADER: 210

In this last line you need only eliminate the reference to the third array (ABBREV$(X)).

Third, you may want to modify the way we display the prompt lines—changing the commas between pairs to a dash, for instance:

PROMPT LINES: 29010, 29110, 29240, 29250

You may also want to change the number of characters per input allowed. We set up for a maximum of 14, the number of characters in our longest capital name (Salt Lake City):

PROMPT LENGTH VARIABLE: 190 (PL)

Fourth, we add a CAPITAL NAME and STATE ABBREVIATION on the appropriate side in lines 35030 and 36030.

Fifth, if your data set will have more or fewer than 50 matching sets, or if you modify the number of cheers available for either HUMAN or THE BEAST, you'll want to change the values for the

MATCHING SETS (MS) and the CHEER COUNT (CC) in line 190.

Finally, if you want your array names to be descriptive of what they contain, here are the names and locations of the data array references:

ABBREV$(*): 192, 210, 35030, 36030, 37060
CAPITAL$(*): 192, 210, 555, 645, 655, 800, 35030, 36030, 37060
STAET$(*): 192, 210, 29010, 29110, 29240, 29250, 37060

THE GAME'S CORE: THE RANDOM DATA SCRAMBLER

There are 50 states-and-capitals matching pairs and 20 cheers per side available during each game, but only 10 of each are used (one for each turn). That ensures that each game is unique and keeps things from getting boring for the gameplayer. The Random Data Scrambler routine lives in lines 140–180. It is referenced three times: first by line 230 to choose what 10 matching pairs out of the 50 available will be used, second by line 235 to choose the cheers for HUMAN, and third by line 240 to get THE BEAST's cheers.

```
140  REM RANDOM DATA SCRAMBLER

145  FOR X = 1 TO LIMIT
150  I% = INT (RND (1) * NUM + 1)

155  FOR Y = 1 TO X
160  IF ARRAY(Y) = I% THEN Y = X: NEXT Y:
     GOTO 150
165  NEXT Y

170  ARRAY(X) = I%
175  NEXT X

180  RETURN
```

Here's how it works: lines 145 and 175 define a FOR/NEXT loop that will work LIMIT number of times—in this case, LIMIT is set to 10 in line 190. Each time through the loop, a random number is chosen (line 150) with a value between one and however many data elements are available. The maximum number of available elements will be either 50 (NUM = 50) if we're choosing matching pairs or 20 (NUM = 20) if we're looking for cheers. Lines 155–165 form an inner loop that makes sure the number just chosen hasn't already been selected so that the same matching pair or cheer won't be used twice in the same game. Line 170 stores the random number in ARRAY(*).

After the appropriate number of random numbers has been generated, the program leaves the routine and goes back to pass the numbers to the appropriate array—GAME(*), HUMAN(*), BEAST(*). Then the game can start. The game looks at these numeric arrays to find out what pairs or cheers it's using. Line 540, for instance, says THIS = GAME(HERE), where HERE is a value between one and ten set by the FOR/NEXT command in line 285. Let's say that this is the fifth turn in the game—so that HERE = 5. So THIS = GAME(5). Let's further assume that GAME(5) was assigned the value 27 by the random data scrambler. That means that THIS = 27. Line 550 sends the program to the subroutine at 29000 where the actual pairs are chosen and displayed. What will appear on the screen will be STAET$(27) (see line 29110), which happens to be NEBRASKA (the 27th state in the data set stored in lines 60000–60049).

The random data scrambler may actually be used up to 13 times per game because it is also used each time a gameplayer fails to match a state with its capital (see lines 590–630). We'll leave you to trace the code through yourself.

Feel free to use the random data scrambler as another humanized programming technique in your own programs to avoid repetitious messages. There's nothing more human than avoiding boredom!

Listing II.1: *States and Capitals.*

```
0  REM LAST UPDATE AUGUST 1, 1981
5  REM STATES & CAPITALS BY SCOT KAMINS
10  REM COPYRIGHT 1981 - COMMERCIAL RIGHTS RESERVED
15 :
20  REM HUMAN PLAYS AGAINST COMPUTER.  MACHINE PICKS 10 STATES AT RANDOM.
25  REM HUMAN MUST GUESS THE CAPITAL OF THE STATE SHOWN.
30 :
35  HOME
40  GOTO 190: REM                             STARTUP
45 :
50  REM                                       ANTI-SPLITWORD ROUTINE
55  READ A$:A$ = A$ + " "
60  IF  PEEK (37) > 21 THEN  VTAB 24: HTAB 1: INVERSE : PRINT "PRESS ANY K
   EY FOR MORE (ESC STOPS LIST)";: NORMAL : GET QUIZ$: VTAB 3: HTAB 1: CALL
    - 958: IF QUIZ$ =  CHR$ (27) THEN  RETURN
65  IF A$ = "END " THEN  PRINT TE$: RETURN
70  IF A$ = "PARAGRAPH " THEN  PRINT TE$:TE$ = "": PRINT : GOTO 55
75 A$ = TE$ + A$
80 Y = 0
85 TE$ =  LEFT$ (A$,CT% - Y)
90  IF  LEN (TE$) =  LEN (A$) THEN  GOTO 55
95  IF  RIGHT$ (TE$,1) = " " THEN  GOTO 110
100 Y = Y + 1
105  GOTO 85
110  PRINT  LEFT$ (TE$,CT% - 1)
```

```
115 T =  LEN (A$) -  LEN (TE$)
120  IF T = 0 THEN  GOTO 55
125 A$ =  RIGHT$ (A$,T)
130  GOTO 80
135 :
140  REM                                        RANDOM DATA SCRAMBLER
145  FOR X = 1 TO LIMIT
150 I% =  INT ( RND (1) * NUM + 1)
155  FOR Y = 1 TO X
160  IF ARRAY(Y) = I% THEN Y = X: NEXT Y: GOTO 150
165  NEXT Y
170 ARRAY(X) = I%
175  NEXT X
180  RETURN
185 :
190 PL = 14:MS = 50:CC = 20:LIMIT = 10:ADDER = 0:HS = 0:BS = 0
192  DIM CAPITAL$(MS),STAET$(MS),ABBREV$(MS),BEAST$(CC),HUMAN$(CC)
195  FOR X = 1 TO PL:LINE$ =  CHR$ (95) + LINE$: NEXT X
200 :
205  REM                                        LOAD ARRAYS
210  FOR X = 1 TO MS: READ CAPITAL$(X),STAET$(X),ABBREV$(X): NEXT X
215  FOR X = 1 TO CC: READ BEAST$(X): NEXT X: FOR X = 1 TO CC: READ HUMAN$
     (X): NEXT X
220  GOSUB 30000: REM   TITLE PAGE
230 NUM = MS: GOSUB 140: FOR X = 1 TO LIMIT:GAME(X) = ARRAY(X):ARRAY(X) =
     0: NEXT X
235 NUM = CC: GOSUB 140: FOR X = 1 TO LIMIT:HUMAN(X) = ARRAY(X):ARRAY(X) =
     0: NEXT X
240  GOSUB 140: FOR X = 1 TO LIMIT:BEAST(X) = ARRAY(X):ARRAY(X) = 0: NEXT
     X
245 :
250  HOME
255 HV% = 5:BV% = 5
260 TITLE$ = "STATE CAPITALS": INVERSE : GOSUB 34000: NORMAL
265  HTAB 3: PRINT NAME$;: HTAB 29: PRINT "THE BEAST": PRINT
270  HTAB 6: INVERSE : PRINT "OO";: HTAB 33: PRINT "OO": NORMAL
275 :
280  REM                                        MAIN LOOP STARTS
285  FOR HERE = 1 TO LIMIT
290 TE$ = ""
295 :
400  REM                                        FIRST SHOT
405 ADDER = 10
410  VTAB 22: HTAB 1: CALL  - 868
430 TITLE$ = "-FOR 10 POINTS-"
440  INVERSE
450  GOSUB 34000
460 TITLE$ = "WHAT'S THE CAPITAL OF THE STATE SHOWN?"
470  NORMAL
480  GOSUB 34000
540 THIS = GAME(HERE)
550  GOSUB 29000
555  IF A$ = CAPITAL$(THIS) THEN ADDER = 10: GOSUB 35000: GOTO 820
556 :
557  REM                                        SECOND SHOT
560  VTAB 19: HTAB 1: CALL  - 958
570  PRINT " NO. IT'S ONE OF THESE: ": REM  3 BELS IMBEDDED HERE
580  VTAB 18: INVERSE
590 LIMIT = 3:NUM = MS: GOSUB 140
```

```
600  FOR X = 1 TO 3:HELP(X) = ARRAY(X):ARRAY(X) = 0: NEXT X
610  FOR X = 1 TO 3: IF HELP(X) = THIS THEN X = 3: NEXT X: GOTO 635
615  NEXT X
620 I% =  INT ( RND (1) * 3 + 1)
630 HELP(I%) = THIS
635 SPACE$ = ""
640  FOR X = 1 TO 3: HTAB 25
645 SPACES = CT% -  LEN (CAPITAL$(HELP(X))) - 25
650  IF SPACES > 0 THEN  FOR Y = 1 TO SPACES:SPACE$ = " " + SPACE$: NEXT Y

655 SHOW$ = CAPITAL$(HELP(X)) + SPACE$
660  PRINT SHOW$
662 SPACE$ = ""
665  NEXT X
680  VTAB 22: HTAB 1: CALL  - 958
690 TITLE$ = "FOR 5 POINTS"
700  GOSUB 34000: NORMAL
710 TITLE$ = "TYPE IN ONE OF THE CITIES LISTED"
720  GOSUB 34000
730  GOSUB 29000
800  IF A$ = CAPITAL$(THIS) THEN ADDER = 5: GOSUB 35000: GOTO 820
810 ADDER = 10: GOSUB 36000
820 :
822  IF HERE = LIMIT THEN  GOTO 850
823  VTAB 21: INVERSE : PRINT "RETURN";: NORMAL : PRINT " GETS NEXT STATE"
     : INVERSE : PRINT "C";: NORMAL : PRINT " GETS LIST OF CAPITALS"
     : INVERSE : PRINT "ESC";: NORMAL : PRINT " ENDS THE GAME EARLY"
     : VTAB 22: HTAB 25
824  POKE  - 16368,0: GET QUIZ$: IF QUIZ$ <  >  CHR$ (13) AND QUIZ$ <  >
     CHR$  (27) AND QUIZ$ <  > "C" THEN  PRINT  CHR$ (7): GOTO 823
825  IF QUIZ$ =  CHR$ (27) THEN  HOME : VTAB 13:TITLE$ = "THANKS FOR PLAYI
     NG!": GOSUB 34000: END
826  IF QUIZ$ = "C" THEN  GOSUB 37000
828  VTAB 15: HTAB 1: CALL  - 958
830 :
835 QUIZ$ = ""
840  REM                                        MAIN LOOP ENDS
850  NEXT HERE
860  FLASH
865  VTAB 15: HTAB 1: CALL  - 958
870  IF HS > BS THEN  FOR X = CT% - (1 +  LEN (NAME$) + 5) TO 1 STEP  - 1:
      HTAB X: CALL  - 868: PRINT NAME$" WINS!";: NEXT X: PRINT : GOTO 890:
      REM  BEL IMBEDDED IN LOOP
875  IF HS = BS THEN TITLE$ = "IT'S A DRAW!!": FLASH : GOSUB 34000: NORMAL
     : GOTO 890: REM  10 BELS IMBEDDED HERE
880  HTAB 23: PRINT "THE BEAST WINS!": FOR X = 1 TO 10: FOR RAZZ = 1 TO 10
     :J =  PEEK ( - 16336):J =  PEEK ( - 16336): NEXT RAZZ: NEXT X
890  NORMAL
899 :
900  VTAB 23: HTAB 1: CALL  - 868
910  PRINT "ANOTHER ROUND? (Y/N)";
920  GET QUIZ$
930  IF QUIZ$ <  > "Y" AND QUIZ$ <  > "N" THEN 920
940  IF QUIZ$ = "Y" THEN 960
950  HOME : VTAB 13:TITLE$ = "THANKS FOR PLAYING!": GOSUB 34000: END
960  HTAB 1: CALL  - 868: PRINT "SAME HUMAN? ";
970  POKE  - 16368,0: GET QUIZ$
```

```
980  IF QUIZ$ = "Y" THEN  HTAB 1: PRINT "HANG IN  WHILE I CHOOSE THE STATE
     S...";: GOTO 225
990  GOSUB 30460: GOTO 225
995 :
999  END
1000 :
29000  REM                                         SET-UP & CHECKERS
29010 TITLE$ = LINE$ + ", " + STAET$(THIS)
29020  VTAB 15: HTAB 1: CALL  - 868
29030  GOSUB 34000
29040  VTAB 15
29050  HTAB HT%
29060  INPUT "";A$
29070  IF  LEN (TE$) > 0 AND  LEN (A$) = 0 THEN A$ = TE$
29080  IF A$ = "" THEN  PRINT  CHR$ (7): GOTO 29020
29090  GOSUB 30500: REM  LEAD/TRAIL SPACES
29100 A$ =  LEFT$ (A$,PL)
29110 TITLE$ = A$ + ", " + STAET$(THIS)
29120  VTAB 15: HTAB 1: CALL  - 868
29130  GOSUB 34000
29140  VTAB 22: HTAB 1: CALL  - 958
29150  INVERSE : PRINT "ARE YOU SURE? (Y/N RETURN=Y) ";
29160  NORMAL
29170  POKE  - 16368,0: GET QUIZ$
29180  IF QUIZ$ <  > "N" THEN 29280
29190  VTAB 22: HTAB 1: CALL  - 958
29200  PRINT "PLEASE TYPE IN YOUR NEW ANSWER"
29210  INVERSE : PRINT "RETURN";
29220  NORMAL : PRINT " KEEPS YOUR OLD ANSWER"
29230  VTAB 15: HTAB 1: CALL  - 868
29240  IF  LEN (A$) = PL THEN TITLE$ = A$ + ", " + STAET$(THIS): GOTO 2926
     0
29250 TITLE$ = A$ +  LEFT$ (LINE$,PL -  LEN (A$)) + ", " + STAET$(THIS)
29260 TE$ = A$
29270  GOTO 29030
29280 TE$ = ""
29290  RETURN
29299 :
30000  REM                                          TITLE PAGE
30010  TEXT : HOME :TITLE$ = "STATE CAPITALS":CHAR$ = "*":CT% = 40:L% =  LEN
     (TITLE$)
30070  VTAD 4
30080 HT% = (CT% - L%) / 2 - 1
30090  GOSUB 31000
30100  GOSUB 32000
30110  HTAB HT%: PRINT CHAR$;" ";: INVERSE : PRINT TITLE$;: NORMAL : PRINT
     " ";CHAR$
30170  GOSUB 32000
30180  GOSUB 31000
30190  VTAB 14
30200 RJ$ = "COPYRIGHT 1981"
30210  GOSUB 33000
30220 RJ$ = "BY SCOT KAMINS"
30230  GOSUB 33000
30240 RJ$ = "COML RIGHTS RESERVED"
30250  GOSUB 33000
30260  VTAB 21: HTAB 7: INVERSE : PRINT "RETURN";: NORMAL : PRINT " TO BEG
     IN"
30302  PRINT "PRESS";
```

```
30305  HTAB 7: INVERSE : PRINT "I";: NORMAL : PRINT " TO GET INSTRUCTIONS"

30310  INVERSE
30350  HTAB 7: INVERSE : PRINT "ESC";: NORMAL : PRINT " TO EXIT"
30390  VTAB 22: HTAB 29
30410  POKE  - 16368,0: GET QUIZ$
30415  IF QUIZ$ = "I" THEN  GOSUB 50000: GOTO 30460
30420  IF QUIZ$ =  CHR$ (27) THEN  HOME : VTAB 13:TITLE$ = "STATE CAPITALS
     ": INVERSE : GOSUB 34000: NORMAL : END
30450  IF QUIZ$ <  >  CHR$ (13) THEN  PRINT  CHR$ (7): GOTO 30390
30460  HTAB 1: VTAB 21: CALL  - 958: PRINT : INVERSE : PRINT "PLEASE TYPE
     IN YOUR FIRST NAME & PRESS  THE RETURN KEY: ";: NORMAL : INPUT "";NAM
     E$: IF NAME$ = "" THEN NAME$ = "HUMAN": VTAB 23: HTAB 17: PRINT "HUMA
     N"
30470  VTAB 24: HTAB 1: FLASH : PRINT "JUST A SEC WHILE I CHOOSE THE STATE
     S...";: NORMAL
30498  RETURN
30499 :
30500  REM                                    LEAD/TRAIL SPACES
30510  IF  LEFT$ (A$,1) = " " THEN A$ =  RIGHT$ (A$, LEN (A$) - 1): GOTO 3
     0510
30520  IF  RIGHT$ (A$,1) = " " THEN A$ =  LEFT$ (A$, LEN (A$) - 1): GOTO 3
     0520
30530  RETURN
30999 :
31000  REM                               BOTTOM & TOP LINE FOR BORDERS
31005  HTAB HT%: FOR X = 1 TO L% + 4: PRINT CHAR$;: NEXT X
31040  PRINT
31050  RETURN
31099 :
32000  REM                                    BLANK LINE
32005  HTAB HT%: PRINT CHAR$;: FOR X = 1 TO L% + 2: PRINT " ";: NEXT X
32040  PRINT CHAR$
32050  RETURN
32999 :
33000  REM                                    RIGHT JUSTIFY
33010  HTAB CT% - 1 -  LEN (RJ$)
33020  PRINT RJ$
33030  RETURN
33999 :
34000  REM                                    CENTERING
34010 L% =  LEN (TITLE$)
34020 HT% = (CT% - L%) / 2
34030  HTAB HT%
34040  PRINT TITLE$
34050  RETURN
34999 :
35000  REM                                    HUMANS GET ONE
35010  VTAB 18: HTAB 1: CALL  - 958
35020  FLASH : PRINT HUMAN$(HUMAN(HERE)): NORMAL
35030  HTAB 2: VTAB HV%: PRINT CAPITAL$(THIS)" "ABBREV$(THIS)
35040 HV% = HV% + 1
35050  INVERSE : FOR X = 1 TO ADDER: VTAB 4: HTAB 6:HS = HS + 1: FOR STALL
      = 1 TO 75: NEXT STALL: IF HS < 10 THEN  HTAB 7
35060  PRINT "";: REM BEL
35070  PRINT HS
35080  NEXT X
35090  VTAB 18: HTAB 1: CALL  - 958
```

```
35100  RETURN
35999 :
36000  REM                                       BEAST GETS ONE
36010  VTAB 18: HTAB 1: CALL  - 958
36020  FLASH :RJ$ = BEAST$(BEAST(HERE)): GOSUB 33000: NORMAL
36030  VTAB BV%:RJ$ = CAPITAL$(THIS) + " " + ABBREV$(THIS): GOSUB 33000
36040 BV% = BV% + 1
36050  INVERSE : FOR X = 1 TO ADDER: VTAB 4: HTAB 33:BS = BS + 1: FOR STAL
     L = 1 TO 75: NEXT STALL: IF BS < 10 THEN  HTAB 34
36060  FOR RAZZ = 1 TO 10:J =  PEEK ( - 16336):J =  PEEK ( - 16336): NEXT
     RAZZ
36070  PRINT BS
36080  NEXT X
36090  VTAB 18: HTAB 1: CALL  - 958
36095  RETURN
36999 :
37000  REM                                       CAPITALS DISPLAY
37005  NORMAL
37010  VTAB 15: HTAB 1: CALL  - 958
37020  INVERSE : HTAB 2: PRINT "CAPITAL";: HTAB 18: PRINT "STATE";: HTAB 3
     1: PRINT "(ABBREV)": NORMAL : PRINT
37050  FOR X = 1 TO MS
37060  PRINT CAPITAL$(X);: HTAB 17: PRINT STAET$(X);: HTAB 32: PRINT " ("A
     BBREV$(X);")"
37065  IF  PEEK (37) > 21 THEN  VTAB 24: HTAB 1: INVERSE : PRINT "PRESS AN
     Y KEY FOR MORE (ESC STOPS LIST)";: NORMAL : POKE  - 16368,0: GET QUIZ
     $: VTAB 17: HTAB 1: CALL  - 958: IF QUIZ$ =  CHR$ (27) THEN X = MS: NEXT
     X: GOTO 37085
37070  NEXT X
37080  VTAB 24: HTAB 1: INVERSE : PRINT "PRESS ANY KEY TO GO ON WITH THE G
     AME";: POKE  - 16368,0: GET QUIZ$: NORMAL
37085  VTAB 15: HTAB 1: CALL  - 958
37087 QUIZ$ = ""
37090  RETURN
37999 :
50000  REM                                       DIRECTIONS
50010  HOME : INVERSE : GOSUB 34000: NORMAL : PRINT
50015  GOSUB 50
50020  VTAB 24: HTAB 1: CALL  - 868: INVERSE : PRINT "PRESS ANY KEY TO STA
     RT THE GAME...";: POKE  - 16368,0: GET QUIZ$
50030  RETURN
50999 :
60000  REM                                       CAPITALS & STATES DATA
60001  DATA MONTGOMERY,ALABAMA,AL,JUNEAU,ALASKA,AK
60003  DATA PHOENIX,ARIZONA,AZ,LITTLE ROCK,ARKANSAS,AR
60005  DATA SACRAMENTO,CALIFORNIA,CA,DENVER,COLORADO,CO
60007  DATA HARTFORD,CONNECTICUT,CT,DOVER,DELAWARE,DE
60009  DATA TALLAHASSEE,FLORIDA,FL,ATLANTA,GEORGIA,GA
60011  DATA HONOLULU,HAWAII,HI,BOISE,IDAHO,ID
60013  DATA SPRINGFIELD,ILLINOIS,IL,INDIANAPOLIS,INDIANA,IN
60015  DATA DES MOINES,IOWA,IA,TOPEKA,KANSAS,KS
60017  DATA FRANKFORT,KENTUCKY,KY,BATON ROUGE,LOUISIANA,LA
60019  DATA AUGUSTA,MAINE,ME,ANNAPOLIS,MARYLAND,MD
60021  DATA BOSTON,MASSACHUSETTS,MA,LANSING,MICHIGAN,MI
60023  DATA ST. PAUL,MINNESOTA,MN,JACKSON,MISSISSIPPI,MS
60025  DATA JEFFERSON CITY,MISSOURI,MO,HELENA,MONTANA,MT
60027  DATA LINCOLN,NEBRASKA,NE,CARSON CITY,NEVADA,NV
60029  DATA CONCORD,NEW HAMPSHIRE,NH,TRENTON,NEW JERSEY,NJ
```

```
60031  DATA SANTA FE,NEW MEXICO,NM,ALBANY,NEW YORK,NY
60033  DATA RALEIGH,NORTH CAROLINA,NC,BISMARK,NORTH DAKOTA,ND
60035  DATA COLUMBUS,OHIO,OH,OKLAHOMA CITY,OKLAHOMA,OK
60037  DATA SALEM,OREGON,OR,HARRISBURG,PENNSYLVANIA,PA
60039  DATA PROVIDENCE,RHODE ISLAND,RI,COLUMBIA,SOUTH CAROLINA,SC
60041  DATA PIERRE,SOUTH DAKOTA,SD,NASHVILLE,TENNESSEE,TN
60043  DATA AUSTIN,TEXAS,TX,SALT LAKE CITY,UTAH,UT
60045  DATA MONTPELIER,VERMONT,VT,RICHMOND,VIRGINIA,VA
60047  DATA OLYMPIA,WASHINGTON,WA,CHARLESTON,WEST VIRGINIA,WV
60049  DATA MADISON,WISCONSIN,WI,CHEYENNE,WYOMING,WY
60098 :
60099 :
60100  REM                                        BEAST CHEERS DATA
60101  DATA THE BEAST IS THE BEST,YEA BEAST,TECHNOLOGY FOREVER,CHIPS ARE T
     OPS,SILICON LIVES
60102  DATA THE OLE CIRCUITS ARE COOKIN',GO MACHINE!,HOORAY COMPUTER,WE SA
     LIVATE FOR SILICON,ELECTRONICS EVER ONWARD
60103  DATA TURING TRIUMPHS,HAIL HOLLERITH,WE BRAG FOR BABBAGE,PASCAL PERS
     ISTS,WOZ IS WONDROUS
60104  DATA DATA DEVOURS,3 CHEERS FOR COMPUTERS,HI TECH REIGNS,THE TERMINA
     L IS TERRIFIC,LET'S HEAR IT FOR THE MACHINE
60109 :
60110  REM                                        PEOPLE CHEERS
60111  DATA UP WITH PEOPLE,ANOTHER ONE FOR HUMANITY,PEOPLE OVER POWER SUPP
     LIES,YEA HUMAN,GO PERSON!
60112  DATA MORTALS MAKE IT,WE SHALL OVERCOME,DOWN WITH THE TECHIES,KILL T
     HE BEAST,BEAT THE MACHINE
60113  DATA THE COMPUTER'S ON THE RUN!,DESTROY THE DATABUS,DOWN WITH MACHI
     NES,BOO THE BEAST,HOORAY FOR HUMANS
60114  DATA WHO NEEDS HI-TECH!,PULL THE PLUG ON 'PUTERS,WE'RE THE BEST,RIG
     HT ON HUMAN,OK PEOPLE!
60199 :
60200  REM                                        INSTRUCTIONS DATA
60201  DATA THIS IS A GAME YOU PLAY AGAINST THE COMPUTER.  OBJECT OF THE G
     AME IS TO GUESS THE CAPITAL OF THE STATE DISPLAYED ON THE COMPUTER SC
     REEN.
60202  DATA "IF YOU GUESS CORRECTLY ON THE FIRST TRY, YOUR SIDE GETS 10 PO
     INTS."
60203  DATA PARAGRAPH
60204  DATA "IF YOUR FIRST GUESS IS WRONG, THE COMPUTER WILL SHOW YOU THE
     NAMES OF THREE CAPITAL CITIES.  ONE OF THEM IS THE RIGHT ONE.  IF YOU
      CHOOSE CORRECTLY, YOU GET FIVE POINTS."
60205  DATA PARAGRAPH
60206  DATA BUT IF YOU GUESS WRONG THE COMPUTER (CALLED "THE BEAST") GETS
     TEN POINTS!
60207  DATA PARAGRAPH
60208  DATA "THE COMPUTER WILL CHOOSE 10 STATES AT RANDOM TO PRESENT TO YO
     U, ONE EACH TURN.  AFTER EACH TURN YOU CAN SEE A LIST OF ALL THE STAT
     ES AND THEIR CAPITALS (IF YOU WANT TO)."
60209  DATA PARAGRAPH
60210  DATA THE COMPUTER WILL KEEP SCORE FOR YOU SO YOU CAN SEE HOW YOU'RE
      DOING.  IT WILL ALSO SHOW YOU WHICH ONES YOU GOT RIGHT AND WHICH ONE
     S YOU GOT WRONG - THE ONES AWARDED TO THE BEAST!
60288  DATA PARAGRAPH
60290  DATA  GOOD LUCK!
60300  DATA END
```

APPENDIX III: ELECTRONIC PHONE PAD

This appendix is a living example of how a program manual should be written. It contains the manual for the program Electronic Phone Pad. A listing of the program is in this appendix and it can be entered into an Apple II with 48K and Applesoft. The program itself converts the Apple into a message-taking center that allows messages to be stored, retrieved, sorted, and reviewed. It is designed to be used by a typical secretary in an office environment. The manual for this program is the basis of this appendix. It can be viewed as a basic model for a minimum manual, *sans* cartoons, *sans* clever diagrams, etc. A good manual would be more visual than this one, but we wished to keep it simple.

ELECTRONIC PHONE PAD

Program Operator's Manual

A Sample Program and Manual for

APPLE BACKPACK: Humanized Programming in BASIC

COPYRIGHT INFORMATION

TABLE OF CONTENTS

INTRODUCTION

ELECTRONIC PHONE PAD (EPP) is a telephone-message storage and retrieval program for the Apple II computer. Telephone messages are typed into the computer as they come in and are immediately "filed" into the computer's disk (long-term) memory. Messages cannot be lost and a permanent record of all calls is automatically made. Later on any or all messages can be reviewed or automatically typed, and messages that are no longer needed may be removed from the computer's memory.

EPP can store 250 messages per disk with each message containing seven fields of information (a *field* is a group of data which here includes *date, time, message for, message from, phone, message summary code,* and *full messages* up to 230 characters in length). Messages can be retrieved according to one to five levels of criteria. For instance, using one level you can look for all messages left for a certain person. Using two levels you can look for messages left by a particular person on a particular day. Using three levels, you can have the computer tell you about all messages marked "URGENT" left on a particular day for a specific person.

You can delete old messages either one at a time or in groups and, like the search routine, based on up to five levels of criteria. You can delete all messages for a particular person at the same time, or just those messages from a particular caller, and so on. There are also REVIEW ALL and DELETE ALL options. These options allow you to look at and/or clear out all the messages from a disk at the same time. Messages can be printed as they are entered or they can be printed later as they are needed.

Using the "How To Use It" section in this manual, the computer novice can learn to operate the program in less than one hour. The program features a series of HELP commands allowing constant access to both condensed and expanded operating instructions. Human errors can be corrected immediately.

EQUIPMENT REQUIREMENTS

At minimum the program requires an Apple II computer with Applesoft

BASIC in read-only memory (or Language System on disk) and a single disk drive operating under DOS 3.2. The program may be ''muffined'' to operate under DOS 3.3 with a 20 percent increase in storage capacity (see your DOS 3.3 manual or ask your dealer for help).

EPP is set up to operate with a printer (either parallel or serial with appropriate interface card), although the program can operate without it. If you will *not* be using a printer, then see ''Printer Customizations.'' The printer interface should be plugged into slot one. See ''Printer Customizations'' again if your printer is plugged into some other slot.

BACKUP

EPP is stored on a copyable diskette. *Make a copy of this disk and store away the original.* See your Apple Disk Drive Manual for instructions on how to do this. Use the *copy* for day-to-day operations.

Since we recommend that you use a separate disk for each day the program is used, it's a good idea to make a week's worth of copies at a time. That way the telephone operator can have a full supply on hand. Be sure the copies you make are ''clean'' ones—that is, copies of the program disk that have had no messages written to them yet.

HOW TO USE THE ELECTRONIC PHONE PAD

The following tutorial presents step-by-step instructions on how to use this program. You need never have touched a computer to read and use these instructions. Knowing how to type is helpful, but not required.

To get the most out of this material, you should read it while sitting at the computer. Type the examples into the computer and follow the suggestions as they are made, and you'll be operating this program in a very short time. You can't hurt anything. There's plenty of built-in experiment time. If you're adventurous, you may want to jump right in and mess around on your own. That's perfectly OK since there are plenty of on-screen messages to help you along. This tutorial is written for people who like thorough instruction.

There is an Operations Summary Card listing all the commands and explaining the terms used in this tutorial at the back of the manual. Remember: you can't hurt the computer from the keyboard. Making mistakes won't break anything. The program is very forgiving of errors and is prepared to help you every step of the way.

STARTING FROM SCRATCH

If the computer screen has the words ELECTRONIC PHONE PAD on it and looks like this:

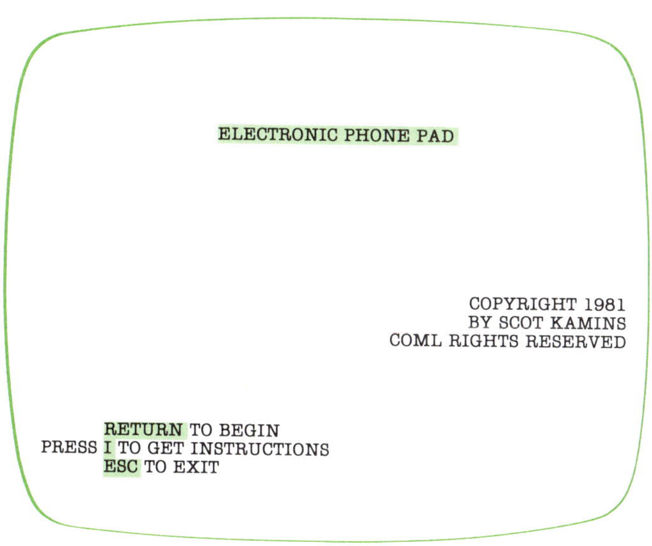

then skip down to ''Starting with the Computer Already On.''

If there's something else on the screen or if the computer isn't on yet, you'll have to get the program ''up and running.'' There are two ways to do this:

1. Scream ''HELP—COMPUTER GONE CRAZY'' until someone comes.
2. Follow the directions in the next few paragraphs.

Method #2 is the preferred way and is really very simple.

Slide the disk labeled ELECTRONIC PHONE PAD into the disk drive. If there are two or more disk drives attached to your system, install the disk in drive #1.

Handle the disk ONLY by the cardboard covering—*don't touch any of the exposed material in the little window*. Make sure the label is *face up and toward you* when you do this (the print will look upside down). The disk will slide all the way in and you should hear a little click or feel a slight grab when it's in all the way. Close the disk drive door.

If the computer is not on, then turn it on by pushing the switch located on the rear left of the machine. Turn on the computer monitor as well. If the disk drive begins to whirr and the little red ''in use'' light comes on, you may skip down to the next paragraph. If the red light on the disk drive does not come on, however, and a star (*) appears to the lower left of the screen, you have an early version of the Apple and you need to do the following:

1. Gently press the number ''6'' on the keyboard and release it. It's the sixth key from the left on the top row.
2. Press the key marked CTRL (the letters stand for CONTROL) and hold it down. It's the first key on the left in the third row down.
3. While you're holding down the CTRL key, press the P key (second row down, third from the right). Now release them both.
4. Press the RETURN key (second row down, first key on the right).

The disk should begin to whirr and the little red ''in use'' light should come on.

STARTING WITH THE COMPUTER ALREADY ON

The EPP is now in memory and running. The first thing to appear on your screen will be the name of the program, copyright information, and a prompt from the computer for you to enter information at the bottom. The prompt (also called a ''cursor'') is the little flashing square of light. It's the computer's way of telling you it wants some information from you, and the program will patiently wait until it gets what it needs.

In this case the computer wants to know what it should do next. It can either begin to accept information about telephone messages, give you abbreviated instructions on how to operate the program (a condensation of what you're reading now), or stop the program entirely.

BEGIN THE PROGRAM

Tell the computer to BEGIN simply by pressing the RETURN key (second row down, first key on the right). If you pressed the ESC key by mistake and the prompt appears next to a '']'' sign, then type the word RUN and press the RETURN key to start again. If you pressed the ''I'' key and a bunch of directions appears on the screen, press the caret (ˆ) key.

Now that you've told the computer to begin the program, it wants to know what you want to begin with. You can work with messages entered before, or you can enter new messages. Since this is the first time you've used the program, we'll assume there are no old messages to look at (we'll come back to this later). Press the N key (N = NEW). If you pressed the R key and got a prompt with the words FIELD # TO SEARCH:, press the caret (ˆ) key to get yourself out of trouble.

ENTERING TELEPHONE MESSAGES

The disk drive will whirr and the beginning screen will be replaced by a screen that looks like this:

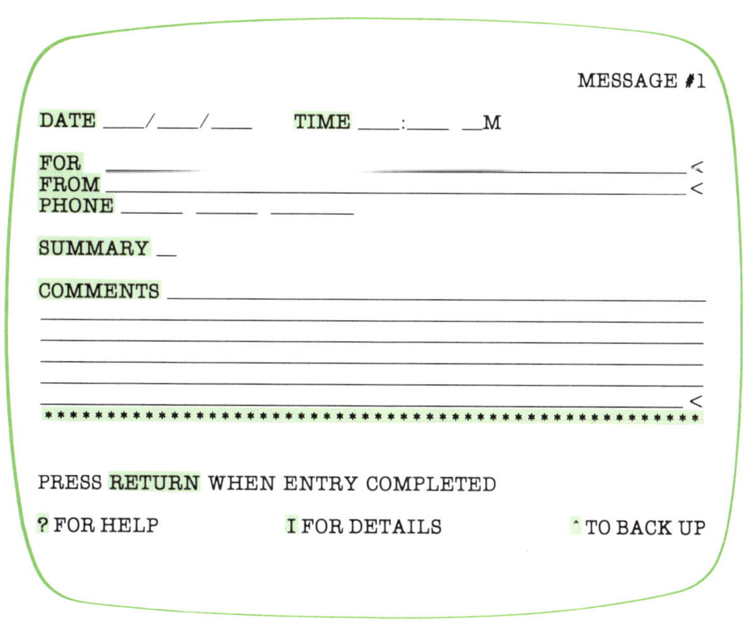

The dashes (—) that you see on the screen represent information that you will supply the computer. There are eight (8) fields (fields are specific areas on the computer screen) in which to supply information to the program. In one field the computer supplies the information automatically. In several fields *all* the dashes must be replaced by information, usually by you, but in other fields (those ending with the < symbol) you determine how much information you'll give the computer. In a couple of places, you can tell the computer to fill in the information it needs from its own memory banks. Clever machine. We'll now explain each field.

1. Message Number

This information is supplied by the computer. It tells you how many messages have been entered for today's date, including this one. Since this is the first message today, it has the number one.

2. Date

Notice that the DATE field is set up with two dashes, a slash, two dashes, another slash, and two more dashes. That indicates the computer wants the date in the form MM/DD/YY where MM represents the month (01 = January, 12 = December), DD is the day (01 = the first day of the month, 31 = the thirty-first day) and YY is the year (82 = 1982). You don't have to type in the slash (/); the computer will do it for you. Type in today's date using this format. Later on you'll see that you only have to type in the date once a day—the computer will remember it for you. If there's already a date in this field, all you need do is press the RETURN key and the computer will keep the date as listed. But since this is the first time you've used the program, you'll have to type it in now. Assume that today is May 1, 1982. Enter the date by typing 05 01 82 (you don't have to type the spaces) and press the RETURN key.

Remember that to the computer the letter "I" is not the same as the number "1" or the lower case letter "l," and the letter "O" is not the same as the number "0." Numbers are on the top row of the computer's keyboard, the letters are in the bottom three rows.

In Case of Trouble

The prompt is now over the first dash in the TIME field. If you find that you've typed in the wrong date and want to go back to fix it, just press the caret key and RETURN and the prompt will move back to the first position in the DATE field. Try it now, just to see how it works. If the date you've typed in is actually OK, there is no need to type it again. Just press the RETURN key and the original date will be accepted by the computer, and the prompt will be positioned over the first dash in the TIME field again.

Help

If you find yourself with the prompt in the first position of a field and you've forgotten what you're supposed to do, press the QUESTION MARK (?) key and RETURN. At the bottom of the page below the line of stars some information will appear telling you what to do. Press it now and see what happens.

If you've forgotten absolutely everything (except this instruction, of course) and, again, the prompt is over the first character in a field, enter the I (for Instructions) key and press RETURN. You'll be presented with all kinds of instructions about the program to jog your memory and help you along.

These various help features will work throughout the program, as long as you press the appropriate key when the prompt is over the first position in any field. Pressing these special keys while the prompt is in another position won't have a disastrous effect on your messages. In fact, nothing much will happen at all. Back to the field descriptions.

3. Time

The TIME of the telephone call should be entered HH:MM where HH is the hour (01 to 12) and MM is the minute (00 to 59). The last dash is for either a (for a.m.) or p (for p.m). The computer will enter the colon and any necessary spaces for you. Assuming that the time is 3:55 p.m., enter the time this way: 03 55 P Once again, the spaces are there just to make it easier for you to read. The computer will ignore them if you type them in. Remember to press RETURN.

4. For Whom

In this field you type in the name of the person for whom the phone call has come. This field is a bit different from the others we've seen. In the first three fields the computer has decided how many characters you need to enter. But here *you* will make that decision. You may enter up to 25 letters. The "<" character at the end of this field marks the twenty-sixth place and is a warning that says "don't type over or past me." If the name of the person for whom the message is being left is longer than 25 letters, you'll have to use some creative abbreviating. Any letters you enter beyond the twenty-fifth will be ignored by the computer when it stores the message to the disk.

This call happens to be for John Scribblemonger, so you'll type in John's name. Don't forget to press the RETURN key when you're done.

If you discover you have made a spelling mistake while you are typing in the name, you may back up over what you have typed by pressing the LEFT-FACING ARROW key (third row down, second key from the right). Each time you press it, the prompt will back up one character. When you have the prompt over your error, type in your correction. Now type out the rest of the name. If all the other letters in the name are correct, you can speed things up by pressing down the RIGHT-FACING ARROW key (third row down, first key on the right) once for each character to be copied. The prompt will copy each character it passes. Try experimenting with these arrow keys by pressing and keeping each of them down (separately, not together) at the same time you press and hold down the REPT key (second row down, second key from the right). The REPT stands for Repeat.

5. From Whom

In this field you type who the caller was. As in the FOR field, you may enter up to 25 letters. For the example we're using, the call is from John's brother, Throckmorton. But we find that the name Throckmorton Scribblemonger is too long to fit within the prescribed limits. So we abbreviate it to Throck Scribblemonger, which fits with room to spare.

6. Telephone

The TELEPHONE field asks that you enter an area code plus a seven-digit number. Throck's number is 415-767-1234. As usual, there's no need to enter brackets, spaces, or dashes; just type the number. Later on you'll see that the computer remembered the last area code you typed, and pressing the RETURN key will type the old area code for you. But since this is the first time you've used the program, you'll need to type it now. If there's an extension number, you should put it at the beginning of the message itself (which you'll type into the COMMENTS field—we'll get to that in a minute).

7. Summary Code

Many times telephone messages say the same things—''please call'' or ''returning your call'' and so on. This field allows you to enter only one keystroke to indicate a summation of a message. To see what your code choices are, enter a question mark (the program's symbol for ''I need help!'') and look at what the computer types below the line of stars.

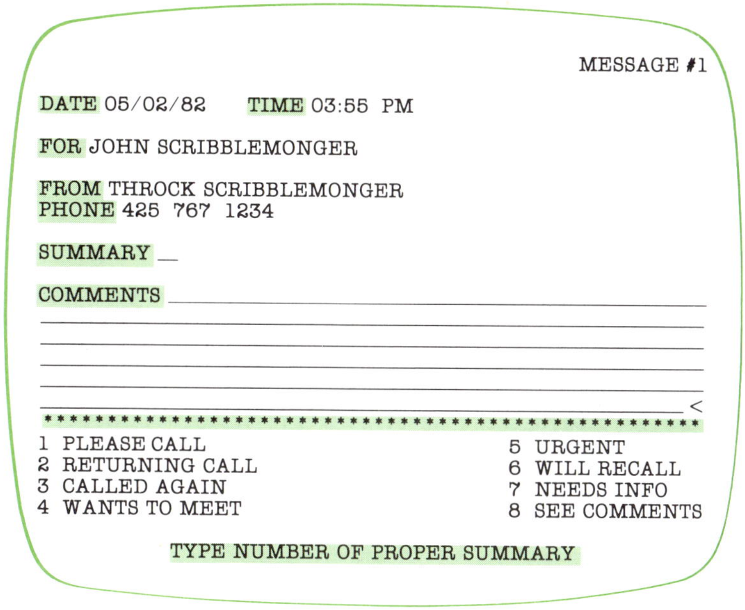

There are eight (8) codes from which to choose. Pressing the RETURN key will cause "SEE MESSAGE," code #8, to be entered in this field. Throck sounds really anxious to talk with John, so you enter code #5. The computer obediently types out "URGENT" for you. That's so you can make sure you pressed the right key. If the message is incorrect, just enter the caret key and type in the correct number.

8. Comments

This is the last field into which you enter information and is where the actual message finally goes. Notice the "< " symbol at the end of the dashes, indicating the "end marker" beyond which you should *not* type. You may enter only up to 230 characters here, so you will need to be brief.

If you press RETURN only as the first character in the field and there are no other characters already in the field, the comment NO MESSAGE will be entered for you by the computer. Mistakes may be corrected via the arrow and REPT keys, as with the FOR and FROM fields. Use your own imagination to decide what the urgent message is that Throck wants to leave for John.

EDIT, PRINT, REVIEW

Now that you've entered a complete phone message, the computer pauses to let you review your work and instruct it what to do next.

```
                                                  MESSAGE #1

DATE 05/01/82     TIME 03:55 PM

FOR JOHN SCRIBBLEMONGER

FROM THROCK SCRIBBLEMONGER
PHONE 425 767 1234

SUMMARY URGENT

COMMENTS FATHER SAYS IF YOU DON'T ALLOW ME TO BORROW
THE MERCEDES FOR MY OUTING WITH CYNTHIA HE SHALL BE
VERY ANGRY!


****************************************************


      P TO PRINT THIS MESSAGE
PRESS RETURN TO ENTER NEXT MESSAGE
      S TO STOP
      R TO REVIEW OLD MESSAGES
      ^ TO BACK UP
```

As you can see from the bottom of the screen, you have several choices. You can print out this message (if you have a printer), enter another message, end the program (either of which choices would cause the disk drive to whirr again, storing the current message to the disk), or review a message already entered. This last choice wouldn't make much sense right now since the message on the screen is the first we've entered.

If you wanted to, you could change (edit) the message currently on the screen by pressing the caret key and then RETURN. If you entered caret several times, the prompt would back up through previous fields of the message—back to the DATE, if you wanted to. And if you then pressed RETURN a few times, all the old information you had entered would be retained as you passed through successive fields again. Try it now, just to prove we're being honest with you.

If there's a printer hooked up to the computer, the machine will type out the entire message on the screen for you. Make sure the printer is turned on and enter P. When the printer gets done typing out the message, you'll have the same choices again. If you need another copy of the message you can type P or you can make some other choice.

Press RETURN and we'll enter another message and examine carry-overs.

LOOKING AT CARRY-OVERS

The screen should look like it did when you first started entering information with two differences. First, the MESSAGE # is now 2, and today's date is already written in the DATE field. If you press the RETURN key now, the computer will automatically accept the current date as correct and move the prompt to the TIME field. In other words, RETURN causes a carry-over condition in the DATE field, keeping the old data carried over from the last message intact.

There is no carry-over value kept in the TIME field because it isn't likely that two calls will come in at exactly the same time. Type in the current time.

As you can see, there is a carry-over in the FOR field. If this new call is for the same person as was the last call, just press RETURN. If it isn't, just type in the new person's name. There's a carry-over here because it's quite possible in a small business that many calls will be for the same person.

There is no carry-over value for FROM. PHONE, however, has a partial carry-over—the area code. It is likely that many calls will be from a local party, so just press RETURN to keep the old area code. The rest of the number, however, has no carry-over. SUMMARY CODE and COMMENTS have no carry-over values (but SUMMARY CODE has a DEFAULT value of "SEE MESSAGE").

REVIEWING OLD MESSAGES

A message pad would be useless if you couldn't read the telephone messages left for you. This section describes how to retrieve the messages you so laboriously entered. When you've finished entering messages, the screen prompts you for your next choice of things to do. Press the R key to tell the computer you want to REVIEW old messages.

The ELECTRONIC PHONE PAD lets you retrieve messages either one at a time or in groups. Depending on how specific you tell the computer to be, you can retrieve any or all messages based on searches up to five (5) levels deep. For example, you can retrieve all messages left for John Scribblemonger. Or you can retrieve all messages left by a specific person. Or, getting even more specific, you can retrieve all messages for John from a specific person on April 3. You choose the combinations you want to search.

The REVIEW screen on your monitor is patiently waiting for you to tell it the FIELD # TO SEARCH: . It wants a number between one and five representing the titles of some of the fields you used when you were entering phone messages. Use the question mark feature to find out what the field names are by just typing the "?" key (the other help features work here, too).

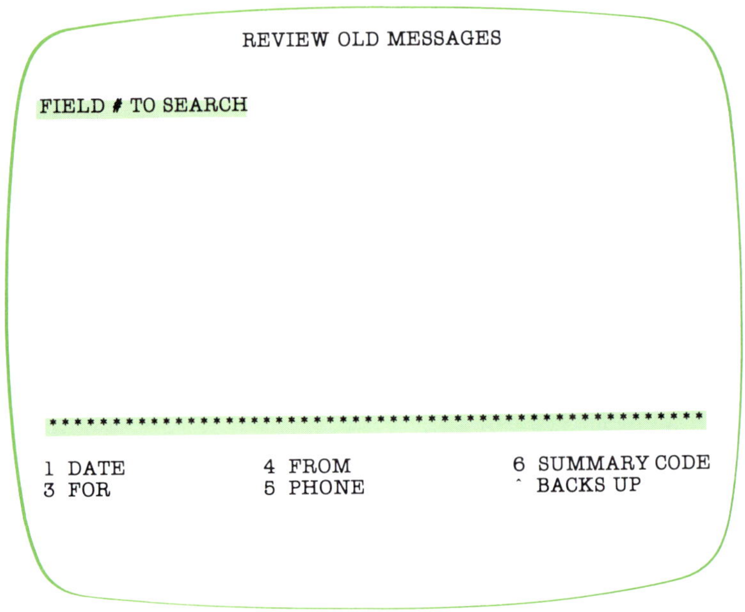

If you wanted to do a search of all the messages on file to see who called a particular person, you'd enter the number two. Do that now.

The computer wants to know whom the calls were for. If you wanted to review all the messages on this disk from the first one entered to the most recent, you would type the word ALL. Assume you want to be more specific than that and type in John Scribblemonger. If this were the only field you wanted to search, you'd enter the number "0" now and the computer would ask you something else. But assume that you don't want all messages on the disk left for John, but just those messages that were urgent. The computer wants to know what SUMMARY CODE you want to search, so enter the question mark key now, and the summary codes will be displayed (unless, of course, you already have them memorized). Choose #5.

If you wanted, you could get more and more specific. But let's assume those are all the restraints you want to make on the computer's search for messages. Enter the number zero.

```
                    SEARCH CRITERIA

3 FOR                  JOHN SCRIBBLEMONGER
6 SUMMARY              URGENT


S SHOWS MATCHES AS THEY ARE FOUND
D DELETES ALL MATCHING MESSAGES
                         S OR D:

*****************************************************

            ^ TO RE-EDIT SEARCH CRITERIA
```

You can order the computer either to show (S) you what it finds or to delete (D) from the disk every message matching the criteria you've set up. This last ability lets you wipe out any messages you have that are no longer wanted or needed. You'll come back to this mass deletion option later. For now choose S.

```
                                        MESSAGE #
DATE                    TIME

FOR JOHN SCRIBBLEMONGER

FROM
PHONE

SUMMARY

COMMENTS




*********************SEARCHING*********************
```

The monitor screen looks like this only *during* a search. It will change when the machine either finds something or runs out of messages. You'll notice that this screen looks a lot like the ENTRY screen. But here only the fields with the search criteria you supplied are filled in. When the machine finds a stored message matching the search criteria you gave it (which by now it should have), it will fill in all the blank fields on the screen.

The number on the bottom of the screen being displayed in black-on-white (known as ''inverse video'' to the technocrats) tells you how many more messages the machine has left to check.

Note that you can't change any of the fields when you use REVIEW. You can't change the past (he said philosophically). But you can wipe it out! The computer gives you the chance to throw this computerized message away (press D for DELETE), to print out this message if you have a printer (press P), to continue looking for more messages that match the criteria you've set (press RETURN), or to abandon the search entirely (press caret). This DELETE concerns only the message displayed on the screen and has no effect whatsoever on the other messages.

MESSAGE #1

DATE 05/01/82 TIME 03:55 PM

FOR JOHN SCRIBBLEMONGER

FROM THROCK SCRIBBLEMONGER
PHONE (415) 767 1234

SUMMARY URGENT

COMMENTS FATHER SAYS IF YOU DON'T ALLOW ME TO BORROW THE MERCEDES FOR MY OUTING WITH CYNTHIA HE SHALL BE VERY ANGRY!

*************THIS IS MATCH #1 OF 1 SEARCH*************

RETURN CONTINUES SEARCH P PRINTS MESSAGE
D DELETES THIS MESSAGE ESC ENDS SEARCH

If you choose to delete the current message, the machine will ask for confirmation from you before it does so—just to make sure you haven't pressed the wrong key! If you confirm, the machine will store the message you've marked for death until all searches are completed and do all its deleting at once. *Warning: Once a message is deleted it is gone forever!*

You may try the PRINT option now if you want (it works exactly the same way it did back in the ''Message Screen Sample'' section), or just press RETURN to see if there are any more messages left for the machine to show you. When it runs out of messages to search, or when you press caret to end the search prematurely, you are faced with more choices. You can either do another review (R), enter more new (N) messages, or end the program (caret).

MASS MESSAGE DELETIONS

At some point you may want to delete all messages for John Scribblemonger, all messages left on June 4, 1981, any messages from Throck Scribblemonger that had summary code #3, and so on. You'd do this to reuse disk space. Use what you've learned to invoke the REVIEW function and you'll see how easy it is.

Essentially, the MASS DELETE function is a variation on the REVIEW function you've been experimenting with. When you see FIELD # TO SEARCH, tell the computer that you want to search for all calls that came in for John Scribblemonger from his brother Throck Scribblemonger. Then tell the machine that those are the only fields you want to specify. Now press D to order the computer to delete all messages matching those criteria. The computer will ask for confirmation to make sure you haven't typed something unintentional. Tell it YES.

```
                    SEARCH CRITERIA


3 FOR               JOHN SCRIBBLEMONGER
4 FROM              THROCK SCRIBBLEMONGER




S SHOWS MATCHES AS THEY ARE FOUND
D DELETES ALL MATCHING MESSAGES

                       S OR D:


****************************************************

PLEASE CONFIRM DELETION OF ALL MESSAGES MATCHING
ABOVE CRITERIA BY TYPING YES AND PRESSING THE RETURN
KEY:
```

Warning: Once a message has been deleted, it's gone forever.

Since these are all practice messages, anyway, in this case we don't care. But when you're dealing with ''live data'' (that is, real phone messages) you'll want to be careful with this option. This is especially true if you had chosen field #2 (FOR) and typed ALL. If you press and confirm D in such a situation, you will wipe out every message on the disk!

FINAL RECOMMENDATIONS

•Use a different disk for each date if you get a lot of calls. That will make REVIEW searches quicker.

•Use the DELETE options only for the most trivial messages. That will keep your records complete.

•Use the SUMMARY CODES often and type COMMENTS only when they are different from the summaries. That will make your fingers last longer.

•To speed up searches in the REVIEW section use as few criteria as possible. For instance, if all messages on the same disk are for the same date, then don't use the DATE as one of the search fields.

•Remember to press RETURN after entering information in each field.

IN CASE OF DISASTER

This program has been designed to eliminate the common causes of ''crash'' due to both programmer and user error. In case the uncommon happens, however, the following emergency measures may help.

RESET

Hitting the RESET key is the single greatest cause of data disaster on the Apple II. Preventive measures should be implemented. Three possibilities, to be done with machine turned *off*, are:

•New Apples have a switch-programmable RESET key. If your machine has this feature, set the switch to CTRL position so that an accidental push of RESET will do nothing.

•Pull the cover off the RESET key. Either place a small rubber washer over the stem or wrap the stem with an elastic band. Replace the cover. This procedure will make it more difficult to press RESET accidentally.

•There are a number of ''RESET protectors'' available commercially that are frequently advertised in the personal computer magazines. Buy and install one.

If a RESET occurs in spite of your best efforts, there are a few things you can do to recover. First, type the word CLOSE and press RETURN. This will protect any data that has already been stored to disk. If the disk drive whirrs, some file was open when RESET was pushed and data may have been lost. Next, find out what the program was doing when RESET was hit. You can probably tell by looking at what's on the screen. If the machine was not either deleting anything or storing a message (in which case the disk drive would have been whirring when RESET happened), no previously stored information was lost. The data still in the computer, however, was clobbered and will have to be re-entered. In most cases that shouldn't take more than a few minutes. If a new message was being typed at the time the RESET occured, then only the new message was lost. If a disk search was in progress no data was lost.

Finally, restart the program (type RUN and press the RETURN key) and do a REVIEW ALL (see ''Reviewing Old Messages'' in the ''How to Use the Electronic Phone Pad'' section) to make sure everything is intact. Checking the last message will let you know if anything disappeared. If the program crashes in this process then your files have been affected and more serious repairs are in order. An accomplished programmer should be consulted.

POWER FAILURE

If you lose power to the computer, then any data in the computer (but probably not on the disk) is gone and unrecoverable. Proceed as in the final step for RESET.

OTHER PROBLEMS

This program works in such a way that any other problems will have trivial negative results. In the worst possible case, only the current message being entered will be lost and the typist will have to re-enter it. Remember that you get out of most tight spots by entering the ^ key (followed by RETURN) when the prompt is in the first position of any field.

PRINTER CUSTOMIZATIONS

If you are not using a printer with this program then you must do the following:

1. Insert the program disk into the disk drive
2. Type ''LOAD ELECTRONIC PHONE PAD''
3. Type ''5 SLOT = 0''
4. Type ''UNLOCK ELECTRONIC PHONE PAD''
5. Type ''SAVE ELECTRONIC PHONE PAD''
6. Type ''LOCK ELECTRONIC PHONE PAD''

If you are using a printer with the interface card plugged into a slot other than slot number one, then you must follow the steps outlined above except for step number 3:

3. Type ''5 SLOT ='' <SLOT WHERE CARD IS PLUGGED>

OPERATION SUMMARY CARD

All definitions used here apply specifically to this program and may not apply to any other.

SPECIAL COMMAND KEYS

Expressions in parentheses tell in what program segment the corresponding key is used.

D—DELETE old message or messages (REVIEW).

I—extended INFORMATION request (first position of any field).

N—enter NEW message (before and after ENTRY or REVIEW).

R—REVIEW one or many old messages (before and after ENTRY or REVIEW).

P—PRINT current message if printer available (ENTRY and REVIEW).

S—SHOW matches to stated criteria as found (SEARCH sequence in REVIEW).

ARROWS—move PROMPT left or right to speed up corrections (ENTRY of FOR, FROM, and COMMENTS fields).

^—back up PROMPT to previous field (works in first position of field). Also used to end current routine.

REPT—REPEAT on screen action of last pressed key (entry of FOR, FROM, COMMENTS fields).

RETURN—begin program (at title page), display and accept DEFAULT or CARRY-OVER data (ENTRY), accept current field, accept previous data moving down page after using a series of ^ options (ENTRY and REVIEW), enter next message (end of ENTRY).

?—request for brief information about current field (first position of any field).

COMPUTER WORDS

Definitions apply specifically to usage within this program but generally apply to most other computer programs. Where two definitions are given the first applies more often.

CHARACTER any letter, number, or symbol that can be typed from computer's keyboard.

CURSOR flashing square of light on monitor screen indicating (1) request by machine for information from typist, (2) position where next typed character will appear.

DATA information to be used by computer, to be stored, or already stored.

DEFAULT (1) result of pressing RETURN without entering other data when requested for information by computer, (2) application of blame (as in ''Default ain't mine, Boss—it's this dumb machine!'').

DELETE eliminate message or messages from computer's memory and from disk. Deleted messages cannot be recovered.

DISK medium that holds computer programs or data.

DISK DRIVE device that takes data from or puts data to a disk.

MACHINE disrespectful appellation for COMPUTER.

MONITOR specialized television used to display information from computer.

PROGRAM (1) sequence of coded instructions that makes a computer work, (2) the program called ELECTRONIC PHONE PAD.

SEARCH look through memory banks for message or messages that match criteria set by typist.

OTHER TERMS

Definitions apply ONLY to this program. Attempts to transfer definitions to similar terms used in other programs may cause extreme disorientation.

CARRY-OVER data from previous message that will become current value for field if RETURN is pressed (a default).

FIELD specific areas on the monitor screen where the typist enters information.

HELP (1) series of special options designed to aid typist including (I), (?), and (ESC), (2) that which typist yells when machine acts strangely.

IN-USE LIGHT little red light in lower left corner of disk drive that comes on when data is being stored or taken from disk.

MESSAGE set of information entered by typist describing a particular call.

TYPIST human currently giving orders to computer through computer's keyboard.

ELECTRONIC PHONE PAD (EPP) PROGRAM DESCRIPTION

Here's a brief description of the major elements of EPP. We've broken it down into four sections. First is an explanation of the various text files EPP uses and how the disk routines operate. Second is a description of the ENTER MESSAGE code; we place emphasis on how special features are accessed. Third comes a section on how the REVIEW MESSAGE code operates with concentration on the SEARCH routine. While SEARCH takes up a very small amount of code (12 lines), it's really the heart of the program. Finally there's a chart of the major subroutines in EPP with references to their line numbers and a description of their functions.

EPP TEXT FILES

EPP uses a total of 18 text files. Ten serial access files are used to hold detailed information on various program functions, seven random-access files contain data generated by the program on each of the seven respective input fields (DATE, TIME, etc.), and one serial-access file holds the current number of messages in disk memory.

Information Files

INFORMATION files are created by the STUFF-IT program from Chapter 4 of *APPLE BACKPACK: Humanized Programming in BASIC*. EPP never writes to these files. They are read by the routine at lines 58000-58340, which gets the file name (assigned to the variable FILE$) from various lines around the program. The file name will be assigned according to the *function* the program user has asked about. There are ten such files in all. All ten have two words in their name as they appear in the disk catalog. The first word is the subject matter of the information—DATE, TIME, etc., and the second word is always INFORMATION. The first field (0) in each file holds the total number of fields to be read. Each field can be from 1 to 239 bytes long.

Input Files

EPP creates seven random-access INPUT files named after the seven fields in each telephone message—Date, Time, For, From, Phone, Summary, and Comments. These are the fields that the SEARCH routine looks at (see below). Each field of a message is stored in the file corresponding to its name (all dates are in the DATE file, all comments are in the COMMENT file, etc.). Record numbers in each file correspond to the message number under which the data were originally entered. Thus message number 27 can be reconstructed by reading record #27 in the files called Date, Time, For, and so on.

All INPUT files are opened at the beginning of the program and remain active until the program is terminated. Occasionally the files are temporarily closed with a CTRL D to prevent them from being written to unintentionally, but the formal CLOSE command is not issued until the program is about to be exited. The files are left OPEN to save time in writing to them, and considerable time is, indeed, saved by this method!

The seven files have different record lengths matching the maximum allowable number of characters per field plus one for the ASCII carriage return code [CHR$(13)] that Apple DOS wants to see at the end of each record. The record lengths for each file are: Date—7, Time—6, For—26, From—26, Phone—11, Summary—2, and Comments—231.

Counter

COUNTER is a serial-access file whose sole purpose is to keep track of how many messages are stored on the disk. The file is read each time the program is *run* and when either the INPUT NEW MESSAGES or REVIEW MESSAGES routines are entered. Each time either of these routines is exited, the COUNTER file is updated so that it always holds the correct number of messages on the disk. If EPP can't find COUNTER on the disk (which usually means the program hasn't been run for the first time), it branches to an ONERR routine at line 25020. This line creates COUNTER and restarts the program.

Storing the Message to Disk

Lines 10100-10130 make up a little FOR/NEXT loop that stores the telephone message to the disk. The array FIELD$(X) (referenced in line 10110) is seven elements long, with each element holding the name of a different input file in numeric order of data input, such as FIELD$(1) = "DATE," FIELD$(2) = "TIME," and so on. As the value of X changes, the name of the file to be written to changes. The value of X also determines what element of the data array ML$(X) in line 10120 is printed to the file. And since all the numbers are in correspondence, the proper data is sent to the proper file and the proper record (N, the referenced record, is the current message number).

HOW "NEW MESSAGES" WORKS

The INPUT NEW MESSAGES loop is located in lines 42–98 while its major code is in a FOR/NEXT loop (FOR ML = 1 TO 7) encompassing lines 50–74. The subroutines called by this loop determine into what field the program operator will enter data. Field #1 is Date, #2 is Time, and so on through #7, Comments. Line 64 sends the computer to the appropriate subroutine to accept the input for the current field.

Each of the seven subroutines called by line 64 is tailored to fit the requirements of a particular input field. For example, field #2, Time (whose routine resides at 200–280), wants two numbers from the user, then puts in a colon, then wants two more numbers, then puts in a space, then wants a letter (either A or P). Field #5, the Phone field, has an entirely different set of needs.

Single Character Check: Accessing Special Features

All seven subroutines call the SINGLE CHARACTER CHECK routine located at lines 20000–20110 if only one character has been entered into a field. The routine looks to see if the character entered is one of EPP's special flags—the carat (ˆ) meaning "jump to first character in previous field for correction," the question mark (?) signaling a call for an explanation, or the letter "I" requesting disk-based detailed information. If the character is one of the flags, then appropriate action is taken—additional flags are set, disk files are loaded, or other subroutines are referenced. If it isn't a flag, the routine sends the computer back "up" to take some other further action (in effect saying "Sorry—not our department." Bureaucracy everywhere!).

After the FOR/NEXT loop at 50–74 has finished, the computer has a completed telephone message in its innards with the seven fields of the message (whose number is stored in the variable N) in an array called ML$(). ML$(1) holds the entered date, ML$(2) holds the time, etc. Lines 76–98 look to see what the program operator wants done with the message (print it out, correct it, store it and end the program, store it and get another message, etc.). Ultimately, unless the operator "dumps" it, the message will be stored to disk via a routine at lines 10080–10160.

HOW "REVIEW MESSAGES" WORKS

REVIEW MESSAGES lives in lines 1000–1680 and some related subroutines. These lines are further broken into several subsections. Lines 1050–1400 accept up to five fields of data upon which to base a search and are looped through up to five times. Many of the same subroutines referenced by the NEW MESSAGES section are called from here, including all the RAM-based HELP routines (1340) and the specialized input routines (1290–1310) needed for the DATE, PHONE, and SUMMARY fields.

Three important variables in this section are FC, FS$(FC), and

FS%(FC). FC, a counter that gets incremented by line 1090, holds the Field Count—that is, the number of fields that will be searched. Since from one to five fields can be established as search criteria, this value can be from one to five. The array FS%(FC) gets its values from line 1250, so that when a field is chosen for a search, its number is set as the value of FS%(FC). FS$(FC) is set in line 1390 and holds the actual data that field number FS%(FC) is supposed to hold if a match is to be found. As we'll soon see, these three variables are used by the SEARCH routine to do its work.

Lines 1410–1470 want the operator to say what to do with the data just entered: change the criteria (1450), search for matches and show them (1470), or delete them as they are found (1480). If MASS DELETE is selected, then lines 1480–1490 want confirmation before the search-and-destroy routines at lines 2600–2765 are summoned.

The SEARCH Routine

The most interesting code in this section occurs in lines 1520–1630, the SEARCH routine. Line 1520 sets up a FOR/NEXT loop (FOR X=1 TO N) to look at every message on the disk (see "Input Files," above). Line 1530 goes to some routines that set up the search display. Line 1540 sets a counter called OK to zero; we'll come back to its purpose in a moment. Line 1550 sets up a nested FOR/NEXT (FOR Y=1 TO FC), using as its upper limit FC or the number of fields that must be searched. In effect, this inner Y loop will look at the appropriate fields within each message named by the outer X loop (X gets the disk "address" of the message while Y looks to see if this message matches the SEARCH criteria).

Line 1570 does all the disk reading by looking at RECORD #X of the file called FI$(FS%(Y)). You'll recall that all seven INPUT files have the same names as the seven input fields and that they have their names stored in an array called FIELD$() in the appropriate order. (Line 1570 abbreviates FIELD$() to FI$(); Applesoft only recognizes the first two characters of a variable name, anyway.) A few paragraphs ago we explained that the array FS%() holds the number of the field to search. Since the input field name is the same as the file name, as Y is incremented so is the reference to the array element in FI$(). Thus the proper disk file is addressed to look for potentially matching data.

Line 1580 pulls the information from the disk into A$. Line 1590 compares the string from the disk with the string the program wants to match (held in FS$(Y)). If there is a match, the counter OK gets incremented and the search goes on, but all elements searched for by the Y FOR/NEXT loop must meet the search criteria. Line 1620 checks to see if *all* fields searched within a particular message match the search criteria. If they do, then various counters get set and the program branches to the subroutine at 2200 to display the message on the screen and to find out from the operator what to do with it. Depending on the operator's answer (see lines 2300–2330) the program will continue the search until X = N; that is, until there are no more messages left to search.

MAJOR EPP ROUTINE LOCATIONS

LINE RANGE	FUNCTION
42 - 98	INPUT messages major loop
100 - 175	DATA input
200 - 280	TIME input
300 - 375	FOR input
400 - 460	FROM input
500 - 584	PHONE input
600 - 645	SUMMARY input
700 - 765	COMMENTS input
1000 - 1680	REVIEW messages major loop
2000 - 2050	SEARCH screen (initial)
2100 - 2125	SEARCH screen (during search)
2200 - 2330	SEARCH screen (match found)
2400 - 2476	HARD COPY printout (PR# SLOT)
2500 - 2540	confirm DELETE MESSAGE
2600 - 2680	do mass DELETE on disk
2700 - 2760	search files to match mass DELETE criteria
3000 - 3070	HTAB positions for PHONE and DATE inputs
10000 - 10060	open 7 DISK files for INPUT material
10080 - 10160	write data to 7 DISK files
10190 - 10220	close all DISK files; update COUNTER file
20000 - 20110	handle single characters from INPUT routines (?,I,^); send to proper subroutine
25000 - 25040	ONERR routines to set up COUNTER file
31000 - 31020	RAM-based DATE HELP accessed via "?"
32000 - 32020	RAM-based TIME HELP accessed via "?"
33000 - 33020	RAM-based FOR HELP accessed via "?"

34000 – 34020	RAM-based FROM HELP accessed via "?"
35000 – 35020	RAM-based PHONE HELP accessed via "?"
36000 – 36050	RAM-based SUMMARY HELP accessed via "?"
37000 – 37020	RAM-based COMMENTS HELP accessed via "?"
50000 – 50150	TITLE PAGE, gosubs to INIT routines, primary choices
51000 – 51090	INITIAL CHOICES from TITLE PAGE routine
52000 – 52060	choose disk-based INFORMATION file from INITIAL CHOICES routine
55000 – 55020	RIGHT JUSTIFY routine
58000 – 58330	DUMP-IT routine for disk-based INFORMATION
59000 – 59090	SCREENPAUSE for DUMP-IT routine
60000 – 60130	INIT data arrays, other variables
61000 – 61070	set up INPUT MESSAGE display form
63000 – 63030	suppress leading and trailing spaces

TEXT FOR THE "HELP" FUNCTIONS

Here's the text we suggest you use for each of the disk-based HELP files. Use the STUFF-IT program from Chapter 4 to create the files (DUMP-IT is built into EPP). Press RETURN whenever you see <CR>. Sometimes you'll see the <CR> in mid-sentence, but that's not really strange since we only have 239 characters per string to work with in the Apple. The text formatter works in 239-character "chunks" and <CR> tells the formatter to process the chunk. If you ignore the <CR> signal, the Apple character-input buffer will overflow and the world will come to an end.

A line with just a "P" in it will flag a new paragraph (that is, tell the formatter not to expect any more characters and cause a blank line to appear on the screen). A line with just "END" in it signifies the end of the file. Section headings (of which there are 10) are to be used as file names, which STUFF-IT will ask for when you've finished entering text for a particular file. Notice that all file names are two words long, and they all end in the word "INFORMATION." All text is shown here in uppercase because the Apple's natural display is all uppercase.

General Information

ELECTRONIC PHONE PAD (EPP) ALLOWS THE TELEPHONE OPERATOR TO KEEP MESSAGES IN A COMPACT AND ORDERLY WAY WITH NO POSSIBILITY OF AN IMPORTANT MESSAGE BEING LOST. <CR>

P <CR>

IN THE PAST TELEPHONE MESSAGES MAY HAVE BEEN WRITTEN ON RANDOM PIECES OF ODD-SIZED PAPER. MESSAGES WERE EASILY MISPLACED OR MISFILED. EPP ENDS ALL THAT. <CR>

P <CR>

BECAUSE OF ITS EXTREME FLEXIBILITY EPP CAN SEARCH OUT MESSAGES FOR SPECIFIC PEOPLE QUICKLY AND EASILY. AND THE PROGRAM CAN BE LEARNED QUICKLY BY ANYONE! <CR>

JUST FOLLOW THE EASY-TO-USE INSTRUCTIONS THAT APPEAR ON THE COMPUTER SCREEN. <CR>

P <CR>

EPP HAS BEEN WRITTEN WITH THE COMPLETE COMPUTER NOVICE IN MIND. IT HAS A BUILT-IN TUTORIAL THAT MAKES IT FUN TO LEARN. <CR>

P <CR>

GOOD LUCK USING EPP—WE KNOW YOU'LL WONDER HOW YOU EVER GOT ALONG WITHOUT IT! <CR>

END <CR>

New Information

PRESSING "N" BRINGS YOU TO THE SECTION OF THE PROGRAM WHERE YOU ENTER TELEPHONE MESSAGES. YOU WILL USE THIS SECTION MOST FREQUENTLY. <CR>

P <CR>

YOU WILL BE ASKED FOR THE FOLLOWING INFORMATION IN THE FOLLOWING ORDER: TODAY'S DATE, TIME OF CALL, NAME OF PERSON FOR WHOM CALL HAS COME, NAME OF THE CALLER, CALLER'S PHONE NUMBER, <CR>

A SUMMARY MESSAGE (BASED ON A LIST OF CODES FOR WHICH YOU CAN GET AN EXPLANATION BY TYPING A QUESTION MARK), AND A DETAILED MESSAGE OF UP TO 230 CHARACTERS. <CR>

END <CR>

Review Information

THIS IS THE SECTION OF THE PROGRAM THAT ALLOWS YOU TO SEE WHAT MESSAGES HAVE BEEN FILED AWAY. <CR>

P <CR>

YOU MAY RECALL MESSAGES BASED ON FROM ONE TO FIVE SETS OF CRITERIA. SUCH CRITERIA MAY INCLUDE ONE OR MORE OF THE FOLLOWING: DATE OF CALL, WHOM CALL WAS FOR, CALLING PARTY, <CR>

CALLER'S PHONE NUMBER AND/OR THE SUMMARY CODE CHOSEN. <CR>

P <CR>

MESSAGES THAT MATCH THE STATED CRITERIA MAY BE DISPLAYED ON SCREEN, PRINTED OUT ON PAPER, OR DELETED. MESSAGES MAY BE DELETED EITHER ONE AT A TIME OR AS A GROUP. <CR>

P <CR>

END <CR>

Date Information

IN THIS FIELD YOU WILL ENTER SIX NUMBERS CORRESPONDING TO TODAY'S DATE. YOU NEED TO ENTER THE INFORMATION IN THE FORM MM/DD/YY WHERE MM MEANS THE MONTH, DD MEANS THE DAY OF THE MONTH, <CR>

AND YY MEANS THE LAST TWO DIGITS IN THE YEAR. IF TODAY WERE JANUARY 3 1986 YOU WOULD ENTER THE NUMBER 01 03 86. <CR>

P <CR>

THE COMPUTER WILL ENTER THE SPACES FOR YOU; ALL YOU NEED ENTER ARE THE NUMBERS. IF YOU FIND THAT YOU'VE MADE A MISTAKE AFTER YOU'VE ENTERED THE DATE, JUST PRESS THE CARET KEY ("^") FOLLOWED BY THE RETURN KEY.

<CR>

P <CR>

THE COMPUTER WILL KEEP IN ITS MEMORY THE LAST DATE ENTERED. IF THE DATE THAT APPEARS ON THE SCREEN IS THE CORRECT CURRENT DATE, MERELY PRESS THE RETURN KEY AND THE COMPUTER WILL ASSUME THE OLD DATE IS CORRECT. <CR>

END <CR>

Time Information

ENTER THE TIME OF DAY BASED ON A TWELVE-HOUR CLOCK. ONE-FIFTEEN IN THE MORNING (01:15 AM) SHOULD BE ENTERED AS 01 15 A. THE COMPUTER WILL TYPE THE COLON AND THE ''M'' FOR YOU. <CR>

P <CR>

IF YOU DISCOVER THAT THE TIME YOU HAVE ENTERED IS WRONG PRESS THE CARET KEY (''^ '') AND THE COMPUTER WILL SET THINGS UP SO THAT YOU CAN JUST RETYPE THE TIME. <CR>

END <CR>

For Information

FOR WHOM IS THIS MESSAGE BEING LEFT? YOU MAY ENTER UP TO 25 CHARACTERS HERE; ALL CHARACTERS BEYOND THE 25TH WILL BE LOST. YOU MAY TYPE TO, BUT NOT BEYOND, THE END MARKER (''<''). <CR>

P <CR>

IF YOU MAKE AN ERROR WHILE TYPING IN THE NAME BUT YOU HAVE NOT YET PRESSED RETURN YOU CAN USE THE LEFT ARROW KEY TO BACK UP TO YOUR MISTAKE AND CORRECT IT. <CR>

END <CR>

From Information

WHAT IS THE NAME OF THE CALLING PARTY? YOU MAY ENTER UP TO 25 CHARACTERS HERE; ALL CHARACTERS BEYOND THE 25TH WILL BE LOST. YOU MAY TYPE TO, BUT NOT BEYOND, THE END MARKER (''<''). <CR>

P <CR>

IF YOU MAKE AN ERROR WHILE TYPING IN THE NAME BUT YOU HAVE NOT YET PRESSED RETURN, YOU CAN USE THE LEFT ARROW KEY TO BACK UP TO YOUR MISTAKE AND CORRECT IT. <CR>

END <CR>

Phone Information

THE TELEPHONE NUMBER REQUIRES TEN DIGITS. THE FIRST THREE ARE THE AREA CODE. AFTER A CODE HAS BEEN ENTERED ONCE THE SAME CODE CAN BE USED FOR SUBSEQUENT PHONE NUMBERS <CR>

IF THE RETURN KEY IS PRESSED AT THE FIRST CHARACTER ENTRY POSITION. <CR>
P <CR>

THE NEXT THREE DIGITS ARE THE CALLING PREFIX AND THE LAST FOUR DIGITS ARE THE NUMBER. <CR>

P <CR>

THUS IF THE CALL IS COMING FROM SAN FRANCISCO THE NUMBER MIGHT BE 415 555 1212 (THE COMPUTER WILL TYPE IN THE SPACES—YOU JUST NEED TO TYPE IN THE NUMBERS). <CR>

IF THE NEXT CALL IS FROM THE SAME AREA CODE, JUST PRESS THE RETURN KEY AND 415 WILL BE TYPED FOR YOU. <CR>

P <CR>

IF THE CALLER LEAVES NO NUMBER JUST PRESS THE NUMBER 0 AND THE MESSAGE "NO NUMBER LEFT" WILL BE TYPED FOR YOU. <CR>

P <CR>

CORRECT ERRORS BY TYPING THE CARET KEY ("^") AS THE ONLY CHARACTER IN THE NEXT FIELD; THE COMPUTER WILL BACK UP FOR YOU SO THAT YOU CAN ENTER IN THE PROPER NUMBER. <CR>

END <CR>

Summary Information

MANY TELEPHONE MESSAGES ARE EXACTLY THE SAME AND CONSIST OF PHRASES LIKE "PLEASE CALL" OR "URGENT" OR "WANTS TO SEE YOU." IN ORDER TO SAVE YOU TIME EPP ALLOWS YOU TO ENTER A SINGLE CHARACTER CODE <CR>

SUMMARIZING ONE OF THE EIGHT MOST COMMON MESSAGES LEFT BY CALLERS. <CR>

P <CR>.

TO SEE A LIST OF THESE SUMMARY CODES ENTER THE QUESTION MARK AS THE FIRST CHARACTER IN THE SUMMARY FIELD. <CR>

P <CR>

IF YOU ENTER THE WRONG CODE THEN TYPE THE CARET KEY ("^") AS THE ONLY ENTRY IN THE NEXT FIELD, AND EPP WILL BACK UP AND ALLOW YOU TO CORRECT YOUR MISTAKE. <CR>

END <CR>

Comments Information

COMMENT FIELD MAY BE UP TO 230 CHARACTERS LONG. IT IS HERE THAT ANY INFORMATION NOT RECORDED IN THE REST OF THE MESSAGE MAY BE LEFT. <CR>

P <CR>

REMEMBER TO RESPECT THE SYMBOL ("<") MARKING THE END OF THE FIELD. ANY CHARACTERS TYPED BEYOND THE MARKER WILL NOT BE REMEMBERED BY THE COMPUTER. <CR>

P <CR>

IF YOU MAKE A MISTAKE WHILE TYPING IN THIS FIELD AND YOU HAVEN'T YET PRESSED THE RETURN KEY YOU MAY USE THE LEFT ARROW TO BACK UP TO YOUR ERROR. IF YOU FIND AN ERROR AFTER YOU'VE PRESSED THE RETURN KEY, PRESS THE <CR>

CARET CHARACTER ("^"). EPP WILL BACK UP TO THE TOP OF THE MESSAGE. PRESSING THE RETURN KEY REPEATEDLY WILL MOVE THE PROMPT DOWN TO THE BEGINNING OF THE COMMENT FIELD SO YOU CAN CORRECT THE ERROR. <CR>

END <CR>

A SAMPLE HELP DISPLAY

Here's what will appear on the APPLE screen if someone presses the "I" key when the EPP title page appears:

```
                GENERAL INFORMATION

ELECTRONIC PHONE PAD (EPP) ALLOWS THE TELEPHONE
OPERATOR TO KEEP MESSAGES IN A COMPACT AND ORDERLY
WAY WITH NO POSSIBILITY OF AN IMPORTANT MESSAGE BEING
LOST.

IN THE PAST TELEPHONE MESSAGES MAY HAVE BEEN WRITTEN
ON RANDOM PIECES OF ODD-SIZED PAPER. MESSAGES WERE
EASILY MISPLACED OR MISFILED. EPP ENDS ALL THAT.

BECAUSE OF ITS EXTREME FLEXIBILITY EPP CAN SEARCH OUT
MESSAGES FOR SPECIFIC PEOPLE QUICKLY AND EASILY. AND
THE PROGRAM CAN BE LEARNED QUICKLY BY ANYONE! JUST
FOLLOW THE EASY-TO-USE INSTRUCTIONS THAT APPEAR ON
THE COMPUTER SCREEN.

PRESS ESC TO END OR RETURN TO CONTINUE.
```

In this example, there is more text than will fit on one screen. The person operating EPP has the option of seeing the rest of the information on this subject or of returning to the program. The automatic page formatting is handled by a combination of SCREENPAUSE and WORD-WRAP routines built into EPP.

ELECTRONIC PHONE PAD

Listing III.1: *Electronic Phone Pad.*

```
0  REM ELECTRONIC PHONE PAD
1  REM COPYRIGHT 1981 BY SCOT KAMINS
2  REM ALL RIGHTS RESERVED
3  REM SUPPLEMENTARY PROGRAM TO APPLE BASIC BACKPACK: HUMANIZED PROGRAMMIN
    G
4  REM COPYRIGHT 1981 BY SCOT KAMINS AND MITCH WAITE
5  REM ANY RESEMBLANCE BETWEEN THIS LISTING AND STRUCTURED CODE IS PURELY
    IMAGINARY.
9 :
10  PRINT  CHR$ (4)"MAXFILES 9"
12  ONERR  GOTO 25000
14 IN$ = "X": REM                          THIS MUST BE FIRST VARIABLE IN TA
    BLE SO THAT "INPUT ANYTHING" ROUTINE WORKS
16  TEXT : PRINT D$: GOSUB 50000: REM          (OPENERS)
18  GOSUB 51000: REM                          (OPENING CHOICES)
20 BACK = 0
22 SLOT = 1: REM                             PRINTER INTERFACE
24  IF QUIZ$ <  > "N" THEN  GOTO 28
26 N = N + 1: GOSUB 42: REM                             (NEW MESSAGES)
28  IF QUIZ$ = "R" THEN  GOSUB 1000: REM      (OLD MESSAGES)
30  GOSUB 10210: REM                           (PUT N IN COUNTER FILE)
32 FC = 0: FOR X = 1 TO 7:FS$(X) = "":ML$(X) = "":TE$(X) = "": NEXT X
34  PRINT
38  PRINT D$: GOTO 18: REM                     (RESTART)
40 :
42  REM                                       ENTER NEW MESSAGES
44  REM
46  FOR X = 1 TO 7:ML$(X) = "": NEXT X
48  HOME : GOSUB 61000: REM                   (SHOW INPUT FORMS)
50  FOR ML = 1 TO 7
52  IF RF THEN RF = 0: GOTO 58
54  VTAB 21: HTAB 1: CALL  - 958: PRINT "PRESS ";: INVERSE : PRINT "RETURN
    ";: NORMAL : PRINT " WHEN ENTRY COMPLETED"
56  VTAB 23: INVERSE : PRINT "?";: NORMAL : PRINT " FOR HELP";: HTAB 13: INVERSE
57  PRINT "I";: NORMAL : PRINT " FOR DETAILS";: HTAB 28: INVERSE : PRINT "
    ^";: NORMAL : PRINT " TO BACK UP"
58 VT = VT%(ML):HT = HT%(ML):ML$ = ML$(ML)
60  VTAB VT: HTAB HT
62  IF  LEN (ML$) THEN REPLAY = 1
64  ON ML GOSUB 100,200,300,400,500,600,700
66  IF IN% THEN IN% = 0: GOTO 48
68  IF  NOT BACK THEN ML$(ML) = ML$
70  IF BACK AND ML = 1 AND  NOT  LEN (ML$(ML)) THEN N = N - 1: RETURN
72 REPLAY = 0:BACK = 0
74  NEXT ML
76  VTAB 20: HTAB 1: CALL  - 958: HTAB 7: INVERSE : PRINT "P";: NORMAL : PRINT
    " TO PRINT THIS MESSAGE"
78  VTAB 21: PRINT "PRESS ";: INVERSE : PRINT "RETURN";: NORMAL : PRINT "
    TO ENTER NEXT MESSAGE": HTAB 7
```

```
79   INVERSE : PRINT "S";: NORMAL : PRINT " TO STOP": HTAB 7: INVERSE : PRINT
      "R";: NORMAL : PRINT " TO REVIEW OLD MESSAGES"
80   HTAB 7: INVERSE :: PRINT "^";: NORMAL : PRINT " TO BACK UP";
82   VTAB 21: HTAB 36: POKE  - 16368,0: GET QUIZ$
84   IF QUIZ$ = "P" THEN  FOR Z = 1 TO 7:TE$(Z) = ML$(Z): NEXT : VTAB 21: HTAB
      1: CALL  - 958: POKE 34,20: GOSUB 2400: POKE 34,0: GOTO 76
86   IF QUIZ$ = "^" THEN 50
88   IF QUIZ$ = "?" THEN  GOSUB 20000: GOTO 82
90   IF QUIZ$ = "R" THEN  GOSUB 10080: GOSUB 10210: RETURN
92   IF QUIZ$ = "S" THEN  GOSUB 10080: GOSUB 10210: RETURN
94   IF QUIZ$ =  CHR$ (13) THEN  GOSUB 10080:N = N + 1: GOTO 42
96   IF QUIZ$ = "I" THEN  GOSUB 62000: RETURN
98   GOTO 82: REM

99 :
100  REM                                              DATE INPUT
105  VTAB VT:H = HT
110  IF  LEN (DD$) THEN ML$ = DD$: PRINT  LEFT$ (DD$,2)"/" MID$ (DD$,3,2)"
      /" RIGHT$ (DD$,2);: HTAB HT
115  FOR X = 1 TO 6
120  GOSUB 3000
125  HTAB HT: IF HT = 0 THEN HT = 14
130  POKE  - 16368,0: GET D$(X): IF D$(X) =  CHR$ (8) AND X > 1 THEN X = X
      - 1: GOTO 120
135  IF D$(X) =  CHR$ (13) AND  LEN (DD$) THEN ML$ = DD$: RETURN
140  IF X = 1 THEN IN$ = D$(X): GOSUB 20000: IF BACK THEN  RETURN
145  IF D$(X) <  CHR$ (48) OR D$(X) >  CHR$ (57) THEN 125
150  IF D$(X) =  CHR$ (13) THEN 125
155  PRINT D$(X);
160  NEXT
165 ML$ = "": FOR X = 1 TO 6:ML$ = ML$ + D$(X):D$(X) = "": NEXT
170 DD$ = ML$
175  RETURN
180 :
200  REM                                              TIME INPUT
205  IF REPLAY THEN  PRINT  LEFT$ (ML$,2)":" MID$ (ML$,3,2)" " RIGHT$ (ML$
      ,1)
210  VTAB VT
215  FOR X = 1 TO 4
220  IF  NOT SEARCH THEN  GOSUB 3000:HT = HT + HT%(2) - 6
225  HTAB HT: POKE  - 16368,0: GET D$(X)
230  IF X > 1 THEN 245
235 IN$ = D$(X): GOSUB 20000: IF BACK THEN X = 4: NEXT : RETURN
240  IF D$(X) =  CHR$ (13) AND  LEN (ML$) THEN  PRINT  LEFT$ (ML$,2)":" MID$
      (ML$,3,2)" " RIGHT$ (ML$,1): RETURN
245  IF D$(X) =  CHR$ (13) OR  ASC (D$(X)) < 48 OR  ASC (D$(X)) > 57 THEN
      225
250  PRINT D$(X);
255  NEXT X
260  PRINT " ";
265  GET IN$: IF IN$ <  > "A" AND IN$ <  > "P" THEN 265
270  PRINT IN$
275 ML$ = "": FOR X = 1 TO 4:ML$ = ML$ + D$(X):D$(X) = "": NEXT :ML$ = ML$
      + IN$
280  RETURN
285 :
300  REM                                              FOR  INPUT
305 L = 25
310  IF REPLAY THEN  PRINT ML$;: HTAB HT: GOTO 320
315  IF  LEN (FD$) THEN  PRINT FRM$(3);: HTAB HT: PRINT FD$;: HTAB HT
320  CALL 768:IN$ =  MID$ (IN$,1)
325 IN$ =  LEFT$ (IN$,L)
330  IF  LEN (IN$) THEN 355
335  VTAB VT: HTAB HT
```

```
340  IF  LEN (FD$) AND  NOT REPLAY THEN ML$ = FD$: PRINT FD$: RETURN
345  IF REPLAY THEN  PRINT ML$: RETURN
350  PRINT FRM$(3);: HTAB HT: GOTO 320
355  IF  LEN (IN$) = 1 THEN  GOSUB 20000: IF BACK THEN  VTAB VT: HTAB HT: PRINT
     ML$(3): RETURN
360  GOSUB 63000
365 ML$ = IN$
370 FD$ = IN$
375  RETURN
380 :
400  REM                                          FROM INPUT
405 L = 25
410  IF REPLAY THEN  PRINT ML$;: HTAB HT
415  CALL 768:IN$ =  MID$ (IN$,1)
420 IN$ =  LEFT$ (IN$,L)
425  IF  LEN (IN$) THEN  GOTO 445: VTAB VT%(4): HTAB HT%(4): PRINT FRM$(4)
     ;: HTAB HT%(4): PRINT IN$;: HTAB HT%(4): GOTO 445
430  VTAB VT: HTAB HT
435  IF REPLAY THEN  PRINT ML$: RETURN
440 IN$ = "CALLER LEFT NO NAME": VTAB VT: HTAB HT: PRINT IN$: GOTO 455
445  IF  LEN (IN$) = 1 THEN  GOSUB 20000: VTAB VT%(4): HTAB HT%(4): PRINT
     FRM$(4);: IF BACK THEN  HTAB HT%(4): PRINT IN$;: HTAB HT%(4): PRINT M
     L$(4): RETURN
450  GOSUB 63000: REM                      LEADING, TRAILING SPACES
455 ML$ = IN$
460  RETURN
465 :
500  REM                                          PHONE INPUT
504 X = VT:Y = HT
508  VTAB X: HTAB Y
512  IF REPLAY THEN  PRINT  LEFT$ (ML$,3)" " MID$ (ML$,4,3)" " RIGHT$ (ML$
     ,4);: HTAB Y
516  FOR X = 1 TO 10
520  IF X = 4 THEN  HTAB Y + 4
524  IF X = 7 THEN  HTAB Y + 8
528  POKE  - 16368,0: GET IN$: CALL  - 868
532  IF X > 1 THEN 548
536  IF IN$ = "0" THEN ML$ = "":PN$ = "": VTAB VT: HTAB HT: PRINT " LEFT N
     O NUMBER": GOTO 580
540  IF IN$ =  CHR$ (13) AND  LEN (PD$) THEN PN$ = PD$: PRINT PN$;:X = 3: GOTO
     572
544  GOSUB 20000: IF BACK THEN  RETURN
548  IF X <  > 4 THEN 560
552  HTAB Y + 4
556  IF IN$ =  CHR$ (13) THEN  PRINT  MID$ (ML$,4,3)" " RIGHT$ (ML$,4): RETURN

560  IF X = 7 THEN  HTAB Y + 8
564  IF IN$ < "0" OR IN$ > "9" THEN 528
568 PN$ = PN$ + IN$: PRINT IN$;
572  NEXT
576  CALL  - 868
580 ML$ = PN$:PD$ =  LEFT$ (PN$,3):PN$ = ""
584  RETURN
588 :
600  REM                                          SUMMARY CODE INPUT

605  IF REPLAY THEN  PRINT CODE$( VAL (ML$)): CALL  - 868: VTAB VT: HTAB 9

610  POKE  - 16368,0: GET IN$
615  GOSUB 20000: IF BACK THEN  PRINT CODE$( VAL (ML$(6))): CALL  - 868: RETURN

620  IF IN$ =  CHR$ (13) AND REPLAY THEN  RETURN
625  IF IN$ =  CHR$ (13) THEN IN$ = "8": VTAB VT: HTAB 9: GOTO 635
630  IF IN$ < "1" OR IN$ > "8" THEN 610
```

```
635  PRINT CODE$( VAL (IN$));: CALL  - 868
640 ML$ = IN$
645  RETURN
650 :
700  REM                                          COMMENTS INPUT
705 L = 230
710  IF REPLAY THEN  PRINT ML$;: HTAB HT
715  CALL 768:IN$ =  MID$ (IN$,1)
720 IN$ =  LEFT$ (IN$,L)
725  IF  LEN (IN$) THEN  GOTO 740: REM   VTAB VT%(7): HTAB HT%(7): PRINT F
     RM$(7);: VTAB VT%(7): HTAB HT%(7): PRINT IN$;: HTAB HT%(7): GOTO 740
730  IF REPLAY THEN  VTAB VT: HTAB HT: PRINT ML$: RETURN
735 IN$ = "NO MESSAGE": VTAB VT: HTAB HT: PRINT "NO MESSAGE": FOR Z = 1 TO
     5: CALL  - 868: PRINT : NEXT Z: GOTO 755
740  IF  LEN (IN$) = 1 THEN  GOSUB 20000: IF BACK THEN  VTAB VT: HTAB HT: PRINT
     ML$(7): RETURN
745  CALL  - 868: FOR Z = 1 TO 16 -  PEEK (37): PRINT : CALL  - 868: NEXT
     Z
750  GOSUB 63000
755 ML$ = IN$
760  IF  NOT BACK THEN ML$ = ML$
765  RETURN
770 :
1000  REM                                          SEARCH INPUTS
1020 BACK = 0:SEARCH = 1:FC = 0
1030  HOME
1040  VTAB 1: HTAB 1:I$ = "REVIEW OLD MESSAGES": HTAB 21 -  LEN (I$) / 2: PRINT
     I$
1050  VTAB 4: HTAB 1
1060  INVERSE : PRINT "FIELD # TO SEARCH": NORMAL
1070  VTAB 19: HTAB 1: INVERSE : PRINT STAR$: NORMAL : CALL  - 958
1080  VTAB 24: HTAB 1: CALL  - 868: HTAB 10: PRINT "-ENTER ";: INVERSE : PRINT
     0;: NORMAL : PRINT " WHEN DONE-";
1090 FC = FC + 1
1100 VT = FC + 5
1110  VTAB VT: HTAB 1
1120  GET IN$
1130  IF IN$ = "0" AND FC = 1 THEN  PRINT "": GOTO 1110
1140  VTAB 20: HTAB 1: CALL  - 958
1150  IF IN$ = "?" THEN  VTAB 21: HTAB 3: PRINT "1 DATE";: HTAB 14: PRINT
     "4 FROM";: HTAB 25: PRINT "6 SUMMARY CODE": HTAB 3: PRINT "3 FOR";: HTAB
     14: PRINT "5 PHONE";: HTAB 25: PRINT "^ BACKS UP": GOTO 1110
1160  IF IN$ = "I" THEN FILE$ = "REVIEW INFORMATION": GOSUB 58000: GOTO 10
     00
1170 ML =  VAL (IN$): REM NEED THIS TO GET HELP
1180  VTAB 24: HTAB 4: PRINT "PRESS ";: INVERSE : PRINT "RETURN";: NORMAL
     : PRINT " WHEN ENTRY COMPLETED";
1190  VTAB 4: HTAB 1: CALL  - 868: VTAB VT: HTAB 1
1200  IF IN$ = "0" OR IN$ = "O" THEN FC = FC - 1: GOTO 1410
1210  IF IN$ = "^" AND FC = 1 THEN  RETURN
1220  IF IN$ = "^" THEN FC = FC - 1:VT = VT - 1: VTAB VT: HTAB 14: GOTO 13
     20
1230  IF IN$ =  CHR$ (13) AND FS%(FC) > 0 THEN IN$ =  STR$ (FS%(FC))
1240  IF IN$ =  CHR$ (13) OR IN$ = "2" OR IN$ =  > "7" OR IN$ < "0" THEN  PRINT
     CHR$ (7);: GOTO 1120
1250 FS%(FC) =  VAL (IN$)
1260  PRINT IN$" ";: CALL  - 868: INVERSE : PRINT FIELD$( VAL (IN$));: NORMAL
     : PRINT " ";
1270 HT = 14: HTAB HT: INVERSE : PRINT FRM$( VAL (IN$));: NORMAL : VTAB VT
     : HTAB 14
1280  IF  LEN (FS$(FC)) THEN  PRINT FS$(FC);: VTAB VT: HTAB 14
1290  IF IN$ = "5" THEN  GOSUB 500: GOTO 1350 REM    PHONE
1300  IF IN$ = "1" THEN  GOSUB 100: GOTO 1350: REM  DATE
1310  IF IN$ = "6" THEN  GOSUB 600: GOTO 1350: REM SUMMARY
```

```
1320  INPUT "";ML$
1330  IF  VAL (IN$) = 6 THEN  VTAB VT: HTAB 14: PRINT CODE$( VAL (ML$))
1340  IF ML$ = "?" THEN  ON FS%(FC) GOSUB 31000,32000,33000,34000,35000,36
     000: VTAB VT: GOTO 1270
1350  IF ML$ = "^" THEN  VTAB VT: HTAB 14: PRINT FS$(FC): GOTO 1110
1360  IF IN% THEN  PRINT "";: HOME : HTAB 1:I$ = "REVIEW OLD MESSAGES": HTAB
     21 -  LEN (I$) / 2: PRINT I$:IN% = 0: VTAB 6: FOR Z = 1 TO FC: PRINT
     FS%(Z)" ";: INVERSE : PRINT FI$(FS%(Z));: NORMAL : HTAB 14: PRINT FS$
     (Z): NEXT : VTAB 5 + FC:IN$ =  STR$ (FS%(FC)): GOTO 1270
1370  IF ML$ = "" AND  LEN (FS$(FC)) THEN ML$ = FS$(FC): VTAB VT: HTAB 14:
      PRINT ML$
1380  IF ML$ = "" THEN  VTAB VT: PRINT  CHR$ (7);: GOTO 1270
1390 FS$(FC) = ML$:ML$ = ""
1400  IF FC < 5 THEN  GOTO 1050
1410  VTAB 24: HTAB 1: CALL  - 868: HTAB 8: INVERSE : PRINT "^";: NORMAL :
      PRINT " TO RE-EDIT SEARCH CRITERIA";
1420  VTAB 1: HTAB 1: CALL  - 868: PRINT  CHR$ (7); CHR$ (7);:I$ = "SEARCH
      CRITERIA": INVERSE : HTAB 21 -  LEN (I$) / 2: PRINT I$: NORMAL
1430  VTAB 12: HTAB 1: INVERSE : PRINT "S";: NORMAL : PRINT " SHOWS MATCHE
     S AS THEY ARE FOUND": INVERSE : PRINT "D";: NORMAL : PRINT " DELETES
     ";: INVERSE : PRINT "ALL";: NORMAL : PRINT " MATCHING MESSAGES"
1440  VTAB 16: HTAB 17: CALL  - 868: INVERSE : PRINT "S";: NORMAL : PRINT
     " OR ";: INVERSE : PRINT "D";: NORMAL : PRINT ": ";: GET QUIZ$
1450  IF QUIZ$ = "^" THEN IN$ = QUIZ$: VTAB 12: HTAB 1: CALL  - 958:FC = 0
     : GOTO 1040
1460  IF QUIZ$ <  > "S" AND QUIZ$ <  > "D" THEN  PRINT  CHR$ (7);: GOTO 14
     40
1470  IF QUIZ$ = "S" THEN 1500
1480  VTAB 21: HTAB 1: CALL  - 958: PRINT "PLEASE CONFIRM DELETION OF ALL
     MESSAGES MATCHING ABOVE CRITERIA BY TYPING ";: INVERSE : PRINT "YES":
      NORMAL : PRINT "AND PRESSING THE ";: INVERSE : PRINT "RETURN";: NORMAL
     : PRINT " KEY:";: INPUT "";QUIZ$
1490  IF QUIZ$ = "YES" THEN  VTAB 21: HTAB 1: CALL  - 958:I$ = "DELETING M
     ESSAGES": VTAB 23: HTAB 21 -  LEN (I$) / 2: FLASH : PRINT I$: NORMAL
     : GOSUB 2700: GOTO 1000
1500 C = 0: FOR X = 1 TO N:FM%(X) = 0: NEXT X
1510  REM          WORLD FAMOUS KAMINS SEARCH ROUTINE
1520  FOR X = 1 TO N
1530  GOSUB 2000: GOSUB 2100
1540 OK = 0
1550  FOR Y = 1 TO FC
1560  PRINT
1570  PRINT D$"READ"FI$(FS%(Y))",R"X
1580  INPUT A$
1590  IF A$ = FS$(Y) THEN OK = OK + 1: GOTO 1610
1600 Y = FC
1610  NEXT Y
1620  IF OK = FC THEN C = C + 1:FM%(C) = X: GOSUB 2200
1630  NEXT X
1635 :
1640  PRINT D$
1650  VTAB 21: PRINT "";:I$ = "SEARCH COMPLETED - " +  STR$ (C) + " MATCHE
     S FOUND": HTAB 21 -  LEN (I$) / 2: INVERSE : PRINT I$: NORMAL : VTAB
     23: HTAB 1: CALL  - 958: PRINT "PRESS ANY KEY TO CONTINUE...";: GET Q
     UIZ$: PRINT
1660  HOME : VTAB 13: PRINT "ONE MOMENT PLEASE..."
1670 SEARCH = 0
1680  RETURN
1690 :
2000  REM                                  SEARCH DISPLAY SETUP
2005  HOME
2010  INVERSE
2015  HTAB 26: PRINT "MESSAGE #"
2020  FOR Z = 1 TO 7
```

```
2025  VTAB VT%(Z): IF Z = 2 THEN  HTAB 20
2030  PRINT FI$(Z)
2035  NEXT
2040  VTAB 21: PRINT STAR$
2045  NORMAL
2050  RETURN
2055 :
2100  REM                                     TEMP SEARCH DISPLAY
2105  VTAB 1: HTAB 37: PRINT X
2110  FOR Z = 1 TO FC: VTAB VT%(FS%(Z)): HTAB HT%(FS%(Z))
2115  PRINT FS$(Z): NEXT Z
2120  VTAB 21: FLASH ::I$ = "SEARCHING": HTAB 21 -  LEN (I$) / 2: PRINT I$
     : NORMAL
2125  RETURN
2130 :
2200  REM                                     FILL IN SEARCH DISPLAY
2205  PRINT D$"MON I"
2210  VTAB 1: HTAB 37: PRINT X
2215  FOR Z = 1 TO 7:TE$(Z) = "": NEXT Z
2220  FOR Z = 1 TO 7
2225  PRINT D$"READ"FI$(Z)",R"X
2230  VTAB VT%(Z)
2235  HTAB HT%(Z)
2240  CALL 768:IN$ =  MID$ (IN$,1):TE$(Z) = IN$
2245  IF Z = 1 THEN  VTAB VT%(Z): HTAB HT%(Z): PRINT  LEFT$ (IN$,2)"/" MID$
     (IN$,3,2)"/" RIGHT$ (IN$,2)
2250  IF Z = 2 THEN  VTAB VT%(Z): HTAB HT%(Z): PRINT  LEFT$ (IN$,2)":" MID$
     (IN$,3,2)" " RIGHT$ (IN$,1)"M"
2255  IF Z = 5 AND  LEN (IN$) THEN  VTAB VT%(Z): HTAB HT%(Z): PRINT "(" LEFT$
     (IN$,3)") " MID$ (IN$,3,3)"-" RIGHT$ (IN$,4)
2260  IF Z = 6 THEN  VTAB VT%(Z): HTAB HT%(Z): PRINT CODE$( VAL (TE$(Z)))
2265  NEXT Z
2270  PRINT D$"NOMON I"
2275  PRINT D$
2280  VTAB 21: HTAB 6: INVERSE : PRINT "THIS IS MATCH #"C" OF "X" SEARCH";
     : IF X > 1 THEN  PRINT "ES";
2300  VTAB 23: HTAB 1: PRINT "RETURN";: NORMAL : PRINT " CONTINUES SEARCH
     ";: INVERSE : PRINT "P";: NORMAL : PRINT " PRINTS MESSAGE";: INVERSE
     : PRINT "D";: NORMAL : PRINT " DELETES THIS MESSAGE  ";: INVERSE : PRINT
     "ESC";: NORMAL : PRINT " ENDS SEARCH";
2305  VTAB 22: HTAB 20: POKE  - 16368,0: GET QUIZ$
2310  IF QUIZ$ = "P" THEN  GOSUB 2400: GOSUB 2000: GOSUB 2100: GOTO 2200
2315  IF QUIZ$ =  CHR$ (27) THEN X = N:: GOTO 2330
2320  IF QUIZ$ =  CHR$ (13) THEN 2330
2325  IF QUIZ$ = "D" THEN  GOSUB 2500: GOSUB 2000: GOSUB 2100: GOTO 2200
2330  RETURN
2335 :
2400  REM                                     PRINT MESSAGE
2404  VTAB 23: HTAB 1: CALL  - 958
2408  PRINT "PLEASE TURN ON PRINTER & PRESS ANY KEY"
2412  HTAB 16: PRINT "(";: INVERSE : PRINT "ESC";: NORMAL : PRINT " CANCEL
     S)";
2416  VTAB 23: HTAB 39: POKE  - 16368,0: GET QUIZ$
2420  PRINT
2424  IF QUIZ$ =  CHR$ (27) THEN  RETURN
2428  PRINT D$;"PR# ";SLOT
2432  FOR Z = 1 TO 7: PRINT
2436 IN$ = TE$(Z)
2440  PRINT FI$(Z)"      ";
2444  IF Z = 1 THEN  PRINT  LEFT$ (IN$,2)"/" MID$ (IN$,3,2)"/" RIGHT$ (IN$
     ,2): GOTO 2464
2448  IF Z = 2 THEN  PRINT  LEFT$ (IN$,2)":" MID$ (IN$,3,2)" " RIGHT$ (IN$
     ,1)"M": GOTO 2464
```

```
2452  IF Z = 5 AND  LEN (IN$) THEN  PRINT "(" LEFT$ (IN$,3)") " MID$ (IN$,
     3,3)"-" RIGHT$ (IN$,4): GOTO 2464
2456  IF Z = 6 THEN IN$ = CODE$( VAL (IN$))
2460  PRINT IN$
2464  NEXT Z
2468  PRINT : PRINT
2472  PRINT D$"PR#0"
2476  RETURN
2480 :
2500  REM                                    DELETE MARKERS
2510  VTAB 22: HTAB 1: CALL  - 958: VTAB 23: PRINT "PLEASE PRESS ";: INVERSE
     : PRINT "Y";: NORMAL : PRINT " TO CONFIRM DELETION:";: POKE  - 16368,
     0: GET QUIZ$
2520  IF QUIZ$ <  > "Y" THEN  VTAB 23: HTAB 1: CALL  - 868: FLASH :I$ = "D
     ELETION CANCELLED": HTAB 21 -  LEN (I$) / 2: PRINT I$: FOR Z = 1 TO 5
     00: NEXT Z: GOTO 2540
2530 FM%(C) = 0
2540  RETURN
2550 :
2600  REM                                    DELETETION CHECKER
2610  FOR Z = 1 TO C
2620  FOR X = 1 TO 7
2630  PRINT D$"WRITE "FI$(X)",R"FM%(Z)
2640  PRINT "D"
2650  NEXT X
2660  NEXT Z
2670  PRINT D$
2680  RETURN
2690 :
2700  REM                             SEARCH ROUTINE FOR MASS DELETION
2705  FOR X = 1 TO N
2710 OK = 0
2715  FOR Y = 1 TO FC
2720  PRINT D$"READ"FI$(FS%(Y))",R"X
2725  INPUT A$
2730  IF A$ = FS$(Y) THEN OK = OK + 1: GOTO 2740
2735 Y = FC
2740  NEXT Y
2745  IF OK = FC THEN C = C + 1:FM%(C) = X
2750  NEXT X
2755  GOSUB 2600
2760  RETURN
2765 :
2800  NEXT X
2810  RETURN
2820 :
3000  REM                                  NUMBERS FOR PHONE & DATE
3010  IF X = 1 THEN HT = H
3020  IF X = 2 THEN HT = H + 1
3030  IF X = 3 THEN HT = H + 3
3040  IF X = 4 THEN HT = H + 4
3050  IF X = 5 THEN HT = H + 6
3060  IF X = 6 THEN HT = H + 7
3070  RETURN
10000  REM                                   OPEN FILES
10010  IF OF THEN  RETURN : REM DON'T REOPEN OPENED FILES
10020  PRINT
10030  REM
10040  FOR X = 1 TO 7: PRINT D$"OPEN"FIELD$(X)",L"FIELD%(X): NEXT X
10050  PRINT D$
10060  RETURN
10070 :
10080  REM                                   WRITE THE FILE
10090  PRINT
```

```
10100  FOR X = 1 TO 7
10110  PRINT D$"WRITE"FIELD$(X)",R"N
10120  PRINT ML$(X)
10130  NEXT
10140 :
10150  PRINT D$
10160  RETURN
10170 :
10180  REM                                         CLOSE THE FILES
10190  PRINT
10200  PRINT D$"CLOSE"
10210  PRINT : PRINT D$"OPEN COUNTER": PRINT D$"WRITE COUNTER": PRINT N: PRINT
     D$"CLOSE COUNTER"
10220  RETURN
10230 :
20000  REM                                         SINGLE CHARACTER CHECK
20010  IF  NOT SEARCH THEN  VTAB 19: HTAB 1: CALL  - 958
20020  VTAB VT: HTAB HT
20030  IF IN$ <  > "^" AND IN$ <  > "I" AND IN$ <  > "?" THEN  RETURN
20040  IF IN$ = "?" THEN 20080
20050  IF IN$ = "I" THEN FILE$ = FI$(ML) + " INFORMATION":IN% = 1: GOSUB 5
     8000:BACK = 1: GOTO 20110: REM   VARIOUS DISK-BASED DETAIL FILES
20060 BACK = 1: IF ML > 1 THEN ML = ML - 2
20070  GOTO 20110
20080  ON ML GOSUB 31000,32000,33000,34000,35000,36000,37000: REM  VARIOUS
      HELP DISPLAYS
20090  IF ML = 3 OR ML = 4 OR ML = 7 THEN ML = ML - 1:RF = 1
20100  VTAB VT: HTAB HT
20110  RETURN
20120 :
25000  REM                                         ERROR CODES
25010  IF  PEEK (218) +  PEEK (219) <  > 60110 THEN 25030
25020  PRINT : PRINT D$"OPEN COUNTER": PRINT D$"WRITE COUNTER": PRINT 0: PRINT
     D$"CLOSE COUNTER": CLEAR : GOTO 0
25030  POKE 216,0: PRINT "ERROR #"; PEEK (222)" IN LINE " PEEK (218) +  PEEK
     (219) * 256
25035  IF  PEEK (222) = 0 OR  PEEK (222) > 15 THEN  PRINT "SEE PAGES 81 &
     136 IN APPLESOFT MANUAL": GOTO 25040
25038  PRINT "SEE PAGES 114 & 115 IN APPLE DOS MANUAL"
25040  PRINT : PRINT  CHR$ (4);"CLOSE": PRINT  CHR$ (4);"MAXFILES 3": END

25050 :
31000  REM                                         DATE HELP
31010  VTAB 21: HTAB 1: CALL  - 958: HTAB 8: PRINT "ENTER DATE AS  DD/MM/Y
     Y SO THAT": HTAB 8: PRINT "MAY 1, 1983 IS 05/01/83"
31020  RETURN
31030 :
32000  REM                                         TIME HELP
32010  VTAB 21: HTAB 1: CALL  - 958: HTAB 8: PRINT "ENTER TIME AS HH:MM SO
      THAT": HTAB 8: PRINT "12 NOON IS     12:00 PM AND": HTAB 8: PRINT "2
     IN THE MORN 02:00 AM";
32020  RETURN
32030 :
33000  REM                                         FOR HELP
33010  VTAB 21: HTAB 1: CALL  - 958: PRINT "FOR WHOM HAS THIS MESSAGE BEEN
      LEFT?    ENTER UP TO 25 CHARACTERS.               DO NOT TYPE BEYOND
     THE ";: INVERSE : PRINT "<";: NORMAL : PRINT " MARKER."
33020  RETURN
33030 :
34000  REM                                         FROM HELP
34010  VTAB 21: HTAB 1: CALL  - 958: PRINT "WHO IS THE PERSON WHO IS CALLI
     NG?       ENTER UP TO 25 CHARACTERS.               DO NOT TYPE BEYOND
     THE ";: INVERSE : PRINT "<";: NORMAL : PRINT " MARKER."
34020  RETURN
```

```
34030 :
35000  REM                                              PHONE HELP
35010  VTAB 21: HTAB 1: CALL  - 958: PRINT "ENTER AREA CODE FIRST.": INVERSE
     : PRINT "RETURN";: NORMAL : PRINT " GIVES LAST TYPED AREA CODE.": INVERSE
     : PRINT "0";: NORMAL : PRINT " MEANS " CHR$ (34)"NO NUMBER LEFT" CHR$
     (34)
35020  RETURN
35030 :
36000  REM                                              SUMMARY CODE HELP
36010  VTAB 19: HTAB 1: CALL  - 958
36020  PRINT "1 PLEASE CALL";: HTAB 26: PRINT "5 URGENT": PRINT "2 RETURNI
     NG CALL";: HTAB 26: PRINT "6 WILL RECALL": PRINT "3 CALLED AGAIN";: HTAB
     26: PRINT "7 NEEDS INFO": PRINT "4 WANTS TO MEET";: HTAB 26: PRINT "8
      SEE COMMENTS"
36030  PRINT
36040  INVERSE :I$ = "TYPE NUMBER OF PROPER SUMMARY": HTAB 21 -  LEN (I$) /
     2: PRINT I$;: NORMAL
36050  RETURN
36060 :
37000  REM                                              COMMENTS HELP
37010  VTAB 21: HTAB 1: CALL  - 958: PRINT "WHAT INFORMATION HAS BEEN LEFT
     ?          ENTER UP TO 230 CHARACTERS.             DO NOT TYPE BEYOND
     THE ";: INVERSE : PRINT "<";: NORMAL : PRINT " MARKER."
37020  RETURN
37030 :
50000  REM                                              TITLE PAGE
50010  HOME : VTAB 5:I$ = "ELECTRONIC PHONE PAD": HTAB 21 -  LEN (I$) / 2:
      INVERSE : PRINT I$: NORMAL
50020  VTAB 14:I$ = "COPYRIGHT 1981": GOSUB 55000
50030 I$ = "BY SCOT KAMINS": GOSUB 55000
50040 I$ = "COML RIGHTS RESERVED": GOSUB 55000
50050  IF OF THEN 50100
50060  VTAB 21: FLASH : PRINT "ONE MOMENT PLEASE WHILE I SET THINGS UP": NORMAL

50070  GOSUB 60000: REM  INIT VARIABLES
50080  GOSUB 10000: REM                                   OPEN FILES
50090 OF = 1: REM   SET FLAG TO PREVENT REOPENING FILES
50100  VTAB 21: HTAB 1:: CALL  - 868: HTAB 7: INVERSE : PRINT "RETURN";: NORMAL
     : PRINT " TO BEGIN": PRINT "PRESS ";: INVERSE : PRINT "I";: NORMAL : PRINT
     " TO GET INSTRUCTIONS": HTAB 7: INVERSE : PRINT "ESC";: NORMAL : PRINT
     " TO EXIT"
50110  POKE  - 16368,0: VTAB 22: HTAB 29: GET IN$
50120  IF IN$ = "I" THEN FILE$ = "GENERAL INFORMATION": GOSUB 58000: GOTO
     50000: REM        DISK-BASED INSTRUCTIONS
50130  IF IN$ =  CHR$ (27) THEN  HOME : VTAB 13: HTAB 10: INVERSE : PRINT
     "ELECTRONIC PHONE PAD": NORMAL : GOSUB 10190: PRINT D$"MAXFILES 3": END

50140  IF IN$ <  > CHR$ (13) THEN  PRINT "": GOTO 50110
50150  RETURN
50160 :
51000  REM                                              NEW OR OLD MESSAGES?
51010  IF N = 1 THEN QUIZ$ = "N": GOTO 51090: REM CAN'T REVIEW MESSAGES IF
      NONE THERE!
51020  VTAB 19: HTAB 1: CALL  - 958
51030  HTAB 10: FLASH : PRINT "PRESS": HTAB 15: INVERSE : PRINT "N";: NORMAL
     : PRINT " TO ENTER NEW MESSAGES": HTAB 15: INVERSE : PRINT "R";: NORMAL
     : PRINT " TO REVIEW OLD ONES"
51040  HTAB 15: INVERSE : PRINT "I";: NORMAL : PRINT " FOR INFORMATION": HTAB
     15: INVERSE : PRINT "ESC";: NORMAL : PRINT " TO EXIT";
51050  POKE  - 16368,0: VTAB 23: HTAB 36: GET QUIZ$
51060  IF QUIZ$ =  CHR$ (27) THEN  HOME : VTAB 13: HTAB 10: INVERSE : PRINT
     "ELECTRONIC PHONE PAD": GOSUB 10190: NORMAL : PRINT D$"MAXFILES 3": END

51070  IF QUIZ$ = "I" THEN  GOSUB 52000: GOTO 51000
```

```
51080  IF QUIZ$ <  > "N" AND QUIZ$ <  > "R" THEN  PRINT "": GOTO 51050
51090  RETURN
51100 :
52000  REM                                    INFORMATION CHOICE ON OPEN
     ERS
52010  VTAB 19: HTAB 1: CALL  - 958
52020  PRINT "INFORMATION ON ENTERING ";: INVERSE : PRINT "N";: NORMAL : PRINT
     "EW MESSAGES    OR ";: INVERSE : PRINT "R";: NORMAL : PRINT "EVIEWING
      OLD ONES (";: INVERSE : PRINT "N";: NORMAL : PRINT " OR ";: INVERSE
     : PRINT "R";: NORMAL : PRINT "):       ( )": VTAB 20: HTAB 39: GET QUI
     Z$
52030  IF QUIZ$ =  CHR$ (27) THEN  RETURN
52040  IF QUIZ$ = "N" THEN FILE$ = "NEW INFORMATION": GOSUB 58000: RETURN

52050  IF QUIZ$ = "R" THEN FILE$ = "REVIEW INFORMATION": GOSUB 58000: RETURN

52060  PRINT "?";: GOTO 52000
52070 :
55000  REM                                    RIGHT JUSTIFY
55010  HTAB 39 -  LEN (I$): PRINT I$
55020  RETURN
55999 :
58000  REM                                    DUMP-IT
58010  PRINT
58020 LIMIT = 15: REM  NUMBER OF LINES/SCREEN TO BE DISPLAYED BEFORE GOING
      TO SCREENPAUSE ROUTINE
58030 TC = 39: REM NUMBER OF COLUMNS TO BASE ANTISPLITWORD ROUTINE UPON
58040  HOME
58050 TE$ = "": HTAB 1
58060 I$ = FILE$: HTAB 21 -  LEN (I$) / 2: INVERSE : PRINT I$: NORMAL : PRINT

58070 D$ =  CHR$ (4)
58080  PRINT D$"OPEN"FILE$
58090  PRINT D$"READ"FILE$
58100  INPUT Z: REM HOW MANY STRINGS?
58110  FOR X = 1 TO Z: REM DO LINES XX - YY FOR Z NUMBER OF TIMES
58120  CALL 768:IN$ =  MID$ (IN$,1):A$ = IN$
58130  IF A$ = "P" THEN  PRINT TE$:TE$ = "": PRINT : GOTO 58290
58140  IF  LEFT$ (A$,1) <  > " " THEN A$ = " " + A$
58150 A$ = TE$ + A$
58160 Y = 0
58170 TE$ =  LEFT$ (A$,TC - Y)
58180  IF  LEN (TE$) =  LEN (A$) THEN 58290
58190  IF  RIGHT$ (TE$,1) = " " THEN  GOTO 58220
58200 Y = Y + 1
58210  GOTO 58170
58220  PRINT  LEFT$ (TE$,TC - 1)
58230 COUNT = COUNT + 1
58240  IF COUNT = LIMIT THEN  PRINT D$: GOSUB 59000: IF B$ =  CHR$ (27) THEN
      RETURN
58250 T =  LEN (A$) -  LEN (TE$)
58260  IF T = 0 THEN 58290
58270  IF A$ <  >  CHR$ (13) THEN A$ =  RIGHT$ (A$,T)
58280  GOTO 58160
58290  NEXT X
58300  PRINT TE$
58310  PRINT D$"CLOSE"FILE$
58320  VTAB 22: HTAB 1: CALL  - 958: PRINT "PRESS ANY KEY TO GO ON...";: POKE
     - 16368,0: GET QUIZ$
58330  RETURN
58340 :
59000  REM                                    SCREENPAUSE
59010  PRINT D$: REM                           TEMORARILY CLOSE FILES
59020 COUNT = 0
```

```
59030  VTAB 23
59040  PRINT "PRESS ESC TO END OR RETURN TO CONTINUE ";
59050  POKE  - 16368,0: GET B$
59060  IF B$ =  CHR$ (27) THEN  RETURN
59070  VTAB 2: CALL  - 958: PRINT
59080  PRINT D$"READ"FILE$
59090  RETURN
59100 :
60000  REM DATA STUFF
60010  FOR J = 768 TO 790: READ I: POKE J,I: NEXT J: DATA  162,0,32,117,25
     3,160,2,138,145,105,200,169,0,145,105,200,169,2,145,105,76,57,213
60020  FOR X = 1 TO 7: READ FIELD$(X),FIELD%(X),FRM$(X): NEXT X
60030  DATA    DATE,7,"--/--/--",TIME,6,"--:-- -M",FOR,26,"---------------
     ----------<",FROM,26,"-------------------------<","PHONE",11,"--- ---
      ----",SUMMARY,2,-,COMMENTS,231,<
60040  FOR X = 1 TO 7: READ VT%(X),HT%(X): NEXT X
60050  DATA  3,6,3,25,5,5,7,6,8,7,10, 9,12,10
60060  FOR X = 1 TO 8: READ CODE$(X): NEXT
60070  DATA PLEASE CALL,RETURNING CALL,CALLED AGAIN,WANTS TO MEET,URGENT,W
     ILL RECALL,NEEDS INFO,SEE MESSAGE
60080  FOR X = 1 TO 230:FRM$(7) = "-" + FRM$(7): NEXT X
60090  FOR X = 1 TO 40:STAR$ = STAR$ + "*": NEXT
60100 D$ =  CHR$ (4)
60110  PRINT D$"OPEN COUNTER": PRINT D$"READ COUNTER": INPUT N: PRINT D$"C
     LOSE COUNTER"
60120  DIM FM%(N + 50)
60130  RETURN
60140 :
61000  REM                                        SHOW FORMS
61010  VTAB 1: HTAB 28: PRINT "MESSAGE #"N
61020  FOR X = 1 TO 7
61030  VTAB VT%(X): HTAB 1: IF X = 2 THEN  HTAB 20
61040  INVERSE : PRINT FIELD$(X);: NORMAL : PRINT " "FRM$(X)
61050  NEXT X
61060  VTAB 18: INVERSE : PRINT STAR$: NORMAL
61070  RETURN
61080 :
63000  REM                                        LEADING, TRAILING SPACES
63010  IF  LEFT$ (IN$,1) = " " THEN IN$ =  RIGHT$ (IN$, LEN (IN$) - 1): GOTO
     63010
63020  IF  RIGHT$ (IN$,1) = " " THEN IN$ =  LEFT$ (IN$, LEN (IN$) - 1): GOTO
     63020
63030  RETURN
```

INDEX

More BYTE Books Coauthored by Mitchell Waite

This is just one of four books coauthored by Mitchell Waite and published by BYTE/McGraw-Hill. You'll find the same friendly, easy-to-follow style and user-centered approach in each of the titles listed below. If you enjoyed and learned from this book, you'll certainly find the others in the Waite series equally helpful.

Computer Animation Primer, by Mitchell Waite and David Fox. Another in the ever-popular "Primer" computer book series, this engaging book introduces the exciting world of computer-animated graphics and presents the tools and techniques for creating original animated graphics on your personal computer. The book first describes the theory of animation and the potentials of various products, and then the authors go on to detail the actual programming techniques used in animation, focusing on character set, plotting, player-missile, and scrolling graphics. *Computer Animation Primer* features full-color illustrations and program listings in Atari BASIC and 6502 assembly language.

8086/8088 16-bit Microprocessor Primer, by Christopher Morgan and Mitchell Waite. The new, vastly more powerful 16-bit microprocessors are destined to become the basis for the next generation of personal computers, and this book provides the understanding you need to harness this remarkable advance in technology. Using a comfortable, down-to-earth approach, the authors detail the design and capabilities of the Intel 8086/8088 16-bit microprocessor. Also examined are two 16-bit "coprocessors," the 8087 Numeric Data Processor and the 8089 I/O Processor. In addition, the authors survey the current scene in 16-bit technology, reviewing software and products such as the new 8088-based IBM Personal Computer.

Word Processing Primer, by Mitchell Waite and Julie Arca. The first book of its kind, *Word Processing Primer* focuses on the newly available microcomputer-based text-editing programs. The authors begin with a review of the field, giving a working knowledge of the equipment and programs that make text editors work. A section on text formatting shows you how to control the final appearance of your printed copy, and a review of ancillary software, such as programs that check grammar or spelling and those that generate indexes or personalized form letters, shows the potential for customized applications. The book goes on to tell you what to look for when choosing a word processor, and a mini-catalog compares features, capabilities, limitations, and prices of many of the most popular pieces of software and equipment.